Drags Grizzly

To: len,   april 30, 2008

Kiauk Kyakyit

may you enter into a world of
understanding, acknowledgement,
acceptance and appreciation.

enjoy!

KAKA Natkin Kaaotas

chris Mikesh,

Drags Grizzly

Chris Luke

Kaka Nuⱡkin Kⱡawⱡas

SUNPATH BOOKS

Published by Sunpath Books
P.O. Box 128
Creston, B.C.
V0B 1G0

Cover and book design by Warren Clark

Printed and bound in Canada

National Library of Canada Cataloguing in Publication

Luke, Chris, 1948-
    Drags Grizzly / written by Chris Luke ; illustrated by Wendy Liddle; edited by Betsy Brierley.

ISBN 0-9733163-0-6

    1. Luke, Chris, 1948-. 2. Kutenai Indians—British Columbia—Lower Kootenay Indian Reserve—Biography. 3. Lower Kootenay Indian Reserve (B.C.)—Biography. I. Liddle, Wendy II. Brierley, Betsy III. Title.

E99.K85L83 2003   971.1'62   C2003-902735-X

DEDICATION

This book is dedicated to my family—my wife Cecilia, sons Chris Jr. and Chad, daughters Carie, Casey, and Cherie—who have shared with me the many moments of jubilation, bereavement, frustration, and the many challenges that have come before us.

I give special thanks to the people of Yaqan Nukiy, who made my job enjoyable and controversial at times; and acknowledge those who have shared my journey for a little while and for a long while and who have affected me personally.

I celebrate my connection with the hills and flatlands of the Creston Valley—the land that I respect and love.

ACKNOWLEDGEMENTS

It is with deep appreciation that I recognize the people who have helped me bring *Drags Grizzly* to reality. The recommendations, suggestions, and goodwill have been tremendous. I cannot thank you enough—

Betsy Brierley, who was recommended to me as an editor. I found it a blessing to work with a person who understood my writing, who spent endless time and energy building momentum for me to carry on with the writing and see it to completion.

Wendy Liddle, whom I met through friends and acquaintances and who gained my trust and respect. She prepared the drawing for the book cover and the depiction of my great-grandfather's battle with the grizzly bear.

Warren Clark, a person with a big heart, who willingly accepted the design project without question, a skillful, creative person with an eye for detail.

My friends, who took the opportunity to read the manuscript and constructively helped me put life into the stories for the reader.

A special thank you to my family, who are a big part of this book, and who have encouraged me to stay the course.

Contents

INTRODUCTION

I AM CHRISTOPHER WILFRED SAMUEL LUKE, BORN IN March 1948 in the old Creston Valley Hospital. My parents were Samuel Tamia Luke and Sophie Sam Luke.

I was blessed with being raised at a time when Ktunaxa traditions were still a part of our community lifestyle. At the same time, we were processing the impacts of the government's influences and compulsions. Through partnership with the government, residential schools were established, fragmenting families and communities of the Ktunaxa Nation.

This is the story of my life as a young boy—and then as a young man—growing up in Yaqan Nukiy with all its joys, sorrows, and adversities. I learned its traditions, while struggling to understand the dominant society.

I am presently the elected Chief of the Lower Kootenay Band. I first held this position thirty-three years ago at the age of twenty-two. I reside in the community of Yaqan Nukiy with my wife, children, grandchildren, sister, brother, extended family, and friends.

DRAGS GRIZZLY

I RECEIVED MY TRADITIONAL NAME, DRAGS GRIZZLY, when I was very young. It stems from Great-grandfather Luke, who went out to hunt small game but, instead, triumphed over a grizzly bear.

Personal names among the Ktunaxa were taken from either the mother's or father's side of the family and given at birth. But traditional name-giving was a ceremonial event. Names came to people in dreams, vision quests, sweats, or ceremonial dances. Often a spiritual leader would bestow on a man or woman the name of their guardian spirit. These honourable names were strictly protected as family property. During ceremonial feasts, people showed respect and gratitude when they received their traditional names. Today, the giving of names is practised. People are slowly regaining the knowledge of custom and tradition.

I did not know the story behind my name until I talked with Mr. and Mrs. Eneas Abraham and Moses Joseph, who all lived in Bonners Ferry in northern Idaho. They are no longer with us in this life. I confirmed the story with my uncle, David Luke, who lived eighty-three years and died in 1986. All the stories were similar in description and detail.

Great-grandfather Luke lived in a nomad village near present-day Copeland, Idaho. He had purchased a single-shot 30-30 rifle and three bullets from a trapper to whom he had traded furs, even though he had never used a firearm before. One morning while out checking the game trails, he came across the tracks of a huge grizzly.

His curiosity roused, he followed them and found himself next to a rockslide, above which was a ledge that overlooked the area. By crisscrossing back and forth, he managed to reach the top, where a well-used trail led towards a rock wall. On the trail lay a large fir tree, probably four or five feet in diameter, which he had to straddle in order to reach the other side. Just beyond was a hole in the rock wall. A powerful odour emanated from this den—the smell of grizzly bear.

As my great-grandfather approached the den to have a look inside, a deep growl startled him. He quickly loaded his rifle, aimed into the den, and pulled the trigger. He could hear the grizzly making its way to the entrance, so he stepped back, ejected and reloaded the rifle, and again aimed in the direction of the den. By this time, the bear was in full view. To frighten the grizzly, my great-grandfather fired his second shot over the animal's head. It stood up on its hind legs, shook its head back and forth, and moved towards the source of this trouble.

As with most wild animals, the grizzly has its own rituals. Because the bear is short-sighted and relies on its senses of smell and hearing, it stands on its hind legs and sniffs the air to identify and locate anything that threatens its domain. Then, it stalks the prey.

In this situation, the breeze was blowing toward my great-grandfather. Although the grizzly could not smell the threat, it could hear the noise. Retreating further, Great-grandfather Luke loaded the rifle for the final time and pulled the trigger. Perhaps he meant to hit the bear, but being inexperienced with the rifle, the shot went wide. By this time, he had backed up into the deadfall fir that was in the path; he leaned backwards onto the log and watched as the grizzly walked toward him in an upright position and stood towering over him. The bear bent down and placed its front paws on either side of my great-grandpa, balancing to sniff out the prey from head to foot.

Most predators seek to prevent their prey from resisting or escaping. The great bear opened its jaws, preparing to bite into the neck and head and thus crush the skull. Facing sure death, Great-grandpa Luke grabbed onto the ears of the grizzly bear. The animal shook its head wildly, trying to get rid of the offender, but my great-grandfather hung on, hoping the bear would tire itself out.

Finally, breathing heavily, the bear paused, giving my great-grandfather a chance to pull his long-bladed knife from its sheath. He stabbed the grizzly in the stomach area, searching for the solar plexus, where the chest cavity and ribs separate. He desperately needed to locate the spot and shove the knife upward into the heart of the animal. Blood was running steadily from many stab wounds before he found the spot he was looking for. He plunged in and upward with all the pressure he could manage, twisting the knife inside the bear's heart.

The two struggled for a very long time. Great-grandpa Luke was able to avoid any fatal injury because he had buried himself tightly against the animal's body and held himself there. He was still holding the ears securely when the grizzly finally toppled onto its back. When my great-grandfather decided the threat was over, he released his grasp and checked himself over. Except for the bear's blood, which covered the entire front of his body, he had not suffered any damage.

Drained and weak, he collected his belongings and headed for home, stopping only to drink the cool water from the spring and wash away the blood. On arriving home, he slept for two days. His wife and everyone in the village were wondering why he was sleeping for so long. When he woke up, he told his wife to gather everyone together so he could tell the story.

"If you don't believe me," he told the people, "go and find the grizzly. You will find my shirt there. Skin the bear. Take the meat and share it among you, but bring me the hide and the heart."

When the men found the bear, they saw no bullet holes but several knife cuts, including the fatal wounds to the heart. They divided the meat among themselves but returned the hide and the heart to my great-grandfather. He instructed my great-grandmother to cook the heart and make sure everyone in the household ate a piece of it in a traditional rite to honour the grizzly bear clan.

During the feast, Great-grandpa Luke decreed that his granddaughter, my mother, would name one of her sons Drags Grizzly to commemorate that eventful day. I am honoured to bear the name.

In mind, body, and spirit, I am *KAKA NUⱢKIN KⱢAWⱢAS*.

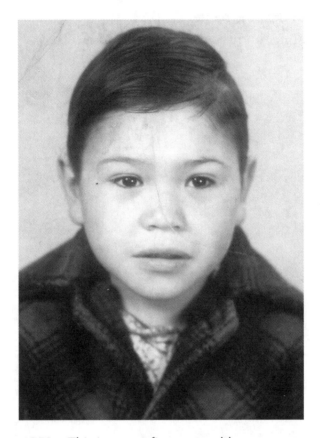

1953—This is me at five years old.

2

GROWING PAINS

LIFE IS FULL OF OBSTACLES. FALLING DOWN AND GETTING back up is how one grows.

It is very difficult to describe the feeling I had when I saw through my own eyes for the first time—like waking up and trying to focus and understand the scenery around me.

I spent my childhood years on the reserves of the Lower Kootenay Indian Band in a small community known as the St. Peter's Mission three miles south of the town of Creston, not far from Cranbrook to the east and Nelson to the west.

Among many fond memories, I recall being inquisitive and trying to be busy around my parents. I remember hanging around the horses. They had just been harnessed and hitched to the wagon and were standing lazily, waiting to get going. In my mischievous and curious way, I climbed into the wagon, unwrapped the reins, and said, "Come on, git up," just the way my dad would say it.

Boy, did the horses respond! They took off in the direction of St. Peter's Church, galloping and in full flight. My mom and dad were hollering at the top of their lungs, chasing after me and the team, shouting "Ho!" The horses roared in behind the church and, luckily, John George heard the commotion and intercepted the team before it headed down the back trail, which eventually met the highway. By that time, I was lying flat on the floor of the wagon, not worrying about where I would end up.

From that day forth, I wore a harness made by my dad and tied to the hitching post with about six feet of cord. Each and every time I tried taking off in any direction, I flipped onto my back, having reached the end of my rope.

Another early memory that stands clear in my mind is the very first time I saw a person other than a member of my family. He was a man who stood very tall. He was staring at me and I was staring back.

Kaⱡa kinʔin? Kakin sakiⱡʔa kakna? "Who are you? What are you doing?" he asked me.

Hu kaʔupxni. "I don't know," I said.

Hun up xni. "I figured so."

I found out later this person was John Alexander, better known to the band members as Big John. He wore braids past his shoulders and a black, broad-brimmed cowboy hat. It wasn't long after that staring match that there was news of his death. He was found floating in the millpond of the Creston Valley Sawmill.

During his funeral, my very first, I witnessed and experienced a part of our forgotten tradition and culture. During the lowering of Big John's casket, a group of women dressed in purple huddled by themselves in the background, wailing away. It seemed they were literally mourning for everyone.

The wailing sound sent chills up and down my spine. I remember glancing back at the women and recognizing my Aunt Nancy, who I believe led the group. The tradition was one of the main ways of releasing grief for loved ones—a custom that is no longer practised. Today, grieving is left up to the individual.

When I think back on that event, it still sends shivers up and down my back. Growing pains are not restricted to the physical being, but to the mental as well.

It is unfortunate that parents somehow deprive children of these unpleasant experiences. Little do we know that it takes these disagreeable circumstances to prepare a child for the ups and downs of adulthood. The reality is that the many roads we travel are rough and unpaved.

As I was growing up, we kids were spared this over-protection. Being five sisters and two brothers of proud, traditional parents, we did little, if any, worrying about one another. When we misbehaved, our punishments were never too severe. Our parents always demanded that we do our best and not leave any mistakes that could be corrected immediately.

My father, whom I called Dad for the longest time, became later known to me as Sam. He was a wrangler, a cattleman who worked on a hay and cattle operation for a rancher who grazed his livestock on the uplands of the Lower Kootenay reservation.

Our father was demanding, which caused some resentment. However, as I became a young adult, I discovered that the high ideals my father made me work for were for my own benefit. He prepared me to cope with the gruelling and sometimes frustrating life of the chief and manager that I came to be.

1953—My mother, Sophie Sam, and father, Samuel Luke.

My mother, Sophie, was a homemaker, taking care of the cooking, wood-chopping, laundry, and housework. On occasion, she would help Dad with feeding, herding, and branding the cattle, mending fences, and especially, assisting with the annual cattle drive into the mountains behind Yahk. She spent her spare time sewing, beading, and making moccasins.

Both my parents had little formal education. It was uncommon to find anyone living on the reserve with more than a grade six education. I grew up in an era in which the language and culture—very strong and much alive—were the focus, mainstay, and livelihood of the people of Yaqan Nukiy, which means "where the rock lies." Today, I speak the Ktunaxa language fluently and am still familiar with most of the customs of our people.

It is unfortunate that the generation after me has lost the

language and tradition. That is not to say that the younger people aren't able to adapt and assimilate. The language and customs are being revived and taught as part of the curriculum in the Band-operated school. It is the hope that, in time, the people of Lower Kootenay will thrive and prosper in their own culture and first language.

As a child of Native ancestry, I carried a certain amount of pride and responsibility. I knew who I was and what my purpose in life was, how to act and talk around grownups. This conditioning prepared me for the world outside the reservation, which I was to face at a very young age.

My first day of school was a disaster. All the disadvantages added up in a hurry. My first language being Ktunaxa, right away I was placed in a handicapped situation because the English language was very hard to understand. I didn't know what was supposed to happen on my first school day; I didn't know the bus schedule and other important details. Little did I know that the first day was for getting acquainted with the teacher and for making friends with the students.

I'm uncertain as to whether or not I made any friends that morning. When the last bell rang, I ran out to the bus yard and looked at all those buses. With all the excitement and trying to remember everything, none of the buses seemed familiar. All the bus drivers wore blue shirts and gray uniforms. Even their faces all looked the same to me. I ended up missing my ride and had walked halfway home before my mother and oldest sister, Clara, met me. Not much was said; however, I was told that I better not let it happen again. I wondered how I could avoid this again if I didn't know what was going on in the first place. What was school all about?

Today I still recognize and feel that little boy's sadness, the empty feelings that cannot be expressed in words.

As time passed, the routine became easier. My English vocabulary and comprehension improved. I made friends. Some remain my friends, although the friends I have today are not what you'd consider perfect, especially when it comes to hanging on to old prejudices.

One of the outstanding memories of my early school days is of my good friend, Linda Robinson. She was like a teacher to me, taking the time to explain things, teaching me the words that the kids were calling me. She even protected me from some of the bullies in school. I got into a lot of fights, the majority of which I didn't instigate. Today I understand why—it was because of my colour and background. The kids in school definitely wanted to knock the Indian out of me. Luckily, Linda was there to make sure that all the odds were even.

Dealing with emotions, your own and others, is probably one of the most difficult things about friendship. I learned at an early age to control, mask, and deny my feelings. Attending school certainly reinforced that denial. And thus, my encounter with racism began.

After that first trial at school, the days that followed were no different. I remember trying to take all my books and scribblers and pencils home. The teacher took a long time to explain why I should leave my things at school for the next day. I got into trouble a lot. I was probably halfway through grade one before I realized that I was being blamed for things the non-Native kids were doing. My punishment was to stand in the hallway or sit on the main steps in the lobby where everyone could see me. Although I thought it was cool at the time, I believe now that the treatment only served to confuse me and contributed to my inferiority complex.

The non-Native children stared at me as if I were different and had done something wrong. Whatever the problem, it manifested in many ways. As in most cases with children, it began with name-calling. They identified me as a "dirty, stinking Indian." I didn't know how in God's creation I could ever fit that description when, in fact, I bathed each and every morning, no matter what the weather was like. Traditionally, children were required to either bathe or swim every day until they reached puberty, until the age of twelve or thirteen.

Fighting became a way of life for me. I was always having to defend myself—to defend who I was, the colour of my skin, my intelligence, and whatever else people said was wrong with me. I can still recall the smirks, the turned-up noses. People would be shocked if I were to name a few of these characters; some of them still act the same as they did twenty or thirty years ago.

When my youngest sister, Doreen, first started school, some of the girls made fun of her. Being a very sensitive person and unaccustomed to the slander, she would often break down crying. I tried to be by her side as much as possible to give comfort. I used to push her on the swings, but one morning a non-Native girl pushed her off. My sister shouted at her in Ktunaxa that she would go home and tell our parents. It really cracked me up.

"Doreen, she doesn't understand a word you are saying. Forget about the swing." I was laughing.

In my fourth year, I moved on to the larger school. The transition was not all that difficult because other students from my community also attended. This arrangement was a treat because we were able to communicate and help one another through the school work.

Grade five was one of the more memorable years because the teachers were magnificent. In the mornings, our teacher was the principal, Mr. Adam Robertson, for whom the school was later named. In the afternoons, Mrs. Nancy Constable taught us. I believe I worked harder in school that year than in all the other years put together. It was the year for music, and I loved to sing. I made the school choir as a soprano, and we practised every Friday before noon.

I especially remember singing "God Save the Queen" at assemblies and concerts. Is it possible that I am not the only one who thought that the Queen was in some kind of trouble? I thought the Queen needed saving and only God could save her. She was sick or old and ready to die, therefore the song required the words: "Long live our noble Queen." The Queen was bitter, sad, and lonely, so: "Send her victorious, happy and glorious, long to reign over us, God save the Queen!" I used to think, poor thing, she's definitely in trouble. I thought if the United States had a man for a president, why did we have a Queen who constantly needed saving? My parents never mentioned to me that the Queen of England was at the head of the Government of Canada.

My love for music had started on the reserve. I danced traditionally; I'd sit around the drum with the elders and listen to the songs they sang and dream of doing what they were doing. My love for drumming became a reality, only it was not the traditional drum that I was beating.

One day I gathered some pots and a garbage can, placed them all around me, and started beating on them, making different sounds and finally combining the sounds which to me sounded beautiful. I was actually making music. I listened often to the radio and began memorizing the songs to play on my pots. I guess you could say my drumming career started then. I remember one afternoon banging away. My father came out and told me to cut the noise, that I was probably irritating the neighbourhood with the "so-called" music. From that time on, I used to tell myself and anyone listening that someday I'd own a set of drums and play professionally.

In the evenings, we enjoyed listening to Elvis Presley music. Adrian Louie was one person I would visit every chance I got, because he used to tell stories, and every once in a while, he would throw a little fiction in to juice it up and we would all be laughing. When I started school, Adrian would watch over me; he showed me how to be a survivor. He was an Elvis Presley fan inside and out. There wasn't another person on the reservation who could match his dedication to Elvis.

During the summer months, at a place we called The Point, above the road to Porthill, Idaho, I spent a lot of time playing a harmonica. It was usually quiet, with very little traffic on the highway in the 1950s. I have a vivid memory of the gophers coming out to stand beside their holes or even move closer, within twenty feet of me, listening to the music.

I recall buying the Rolling Stones' hit single "I Can't Get

No Satisfaction." I would play it on my little turntable over and over and over again. My older sister, Mary Louise, told me to quit playing it so much, but I didn't pay any attention. She finally threatened to take it away and break it. When I still didn't listen, she actually carried out her threat. I was pretty choked; I swore at her and called her every name I could think of. I wasn't thinking about the fact that she had a new baby girl named Josie, her first. Between the baby's whining and my music blaring, her patience level was probably at its lowest. We never spoke of the incident, and we never apologized to each other, although it is still fresh in my mind. I often wonder if this was a source of the friction that always existed between the two of us. Mary passed on in the spring of 2003.

During those first years of school, I had to learn to adjust to a whole new system. As Native people, we believe that everyone and everything is part of Nature and the constant cycle of life. We see the world as a whole; we adjust to the flow of Nature.

Rules and regulations were starting to dominate and control the flow of human life. For example, students had to raise their hands when their name was called during roll call. They had to raise their hands and ask permission to use the washroom. We weren't allowed to answer and move freely, as was our tradition.

Probably, the biggest form of control (or more to the point, segregation and prejudice) took place while we were transported to and from school. During all those years, the

Indian children were told to sit in the back seats of the bus. When the other students threw pieces of eraser or spitballs at us or hurled abuse, we retaliated and then were disciplined by the bus driver, who often made us walk home. My value system was also being forced into the back seat of that bus.

Adjusting my home life to my school life was an added chore, because at this point everything revolved around school. I either had to do things before school or when I returned after school, so I missed out on the annual fishing, hunting, root-gathering, and berry-picking expeditions with my family.

In the fall of 1960 when I moved to the high school, I was thrilled. I felt very important because I had moved ahead to grade seven. But it didn't take long to attract some enemies. Two guys particularly would come around every noon hour to harass me. I would challenge one to a fight, while the other would pepper me with names. There's one that continues to echo in my mind.

"Pieface!"

Then I would retaliate. "Come on, let's fight and I'll turn *your* face into pie!"

Once I ran the guy into the lockers, but didn't get the opportunity to throw any punches because the bell rang for class. I could put names to these two characters, but I'll hold my peace.

The name-calling and intolerance didn't end, and each year it seemed harder to continue going to school. The work was no problem, but the kids were. They seemed to have nothing better to do than criticize. Little did anyone know that the same treatment carried on in my home and in our community. Being lighter skinned than the other Native children, I was labelled "little white boy." It created many hardships for my mother with her friends and relatives. I learned to hate those people who called me "stinking Indian," "redskin," "renegade," "wagon burner," "half-breed," and even "apple Indian." As I got older, I would think of my parents and relatives, all the people who lived in the community, and imagine the name-calling going on long before I was born.

The people I knew had already been stripped of their identity, taken from their homes to residential school, deprived of their language, traditions, and culture. Our village was known as the Indian Mission—in my opinion, a derogatory term. There was no pride in or respect for the community name.

On a positive note, the abuse I experienced in school made me a fighter, a survivor. On the negative side, it could very well have destroyed me emotionally and spiritually.

3

MY MOTHER

FEBRUARY IS THE MOST DREADED MONTH. IT WAS IN February 1962 that I experienced the most difficult loss I had to face as a child—the death of *Kama* (my mother).

She had just celebrated her fifty-first birthday; we acknowledged it without a card or cake. I was thirteen and had just begun to know my mother, to form a bond with her, talk with her, ask her questions. I loved my mother; she was my super mom.

It started out to be a good day with the sun shining and snow on the ground. I was in grade seven at the old Prince Charles Secondary School (later destroyed by fire) and was usually excited about seeing my friends, particularly a girl-friend who was very special to me. We had plans to go to a school dance that weekend, but I hadn't asked my mother about it. My plan was to ask her that evening.

Before I left for the bus, I asked, "Are you going to be home when I get back from school, Mom? I have something important to ask you."

"What is it? Tell me now and I'll have an answer for you by the time you come home."

"No, it can wait until then."

She looked at me with a funny frown. "Okay."

It was that frown that caused me concern. I'd never seen her look so distant. She was usually up-front about things. I thought, Who are you, Mom? I knew she would go to town that day because it was Thursday, and it was her ritual to go to town on Thursdays to do some shopping. I felt a sadness overcome me as I waited for the bus. I knew my mother was going to leave us, but I didn't know it would be the last time I would see her alive. As a child I was spiritually gifted. I could see, hear, feel things that were going to happen.

Several early incidents involving my mother remain with me because of their personal impact on my life. One day, when my mother was sawing wood, a short log rolled on her and broke her leg. I did not understand the hurt or the feelings that she was experiencing. She hollered and winced in pain and told me to go to the house and get help. I don't remember the details, but I believe I did what I was told, because my mother was picked up and taken to the hospital.

My second memory is of my mother and me at home alone. I was about four years old. She was using crutches, probably because of the log incident. She mentioned that we needed bread for sandwiches, I guess because she couldn't stand around on the crutches long enough to make fried bread. I said I would go after some bread, and she told me not to bother. However, I took off on a dead run, not really knowing where I was going. I followed a trail that the older people used, keeping to the west side of the gravelled highway, which is now the paved Highway 21. I finally arrived at the store, a place I'd never been before, telling an old man that my mother had sent me to get bread.

The man must have understood me, because there I was on my way home with two loaves of bread. The strangest thing was that I returned home exactly the same way and on the same side of the road—strange, because I don't remember the trip at all. I believe I was protected by the Creator. I believe the Creator guided me home. The trip must have taken hours, but it seemed like a few minutes.

When I arrived home, my mother was sitting in the open doorway crying. My first thought was that she must have hurt herself again, but she was crying for me, worrying about my safety. She was angry, yet relieved. When I handed her the package and told her where I got it, she gasped, dropped the bread, and gave me a terrified look that I will never forget. Later on, I came to know the owner of that store.

Another time, I remember returning home from town on the wagon. My mother was driving the team, and my sister Clara was sitting with her up front. Somehow, I managed to fall out of the wagon and the rear wheel ran over my left leg.

It happened so suddenly that my immediate reaction was to run after the wagon and jump back in before my mother discovered I was not where I was supposed to be. I tried to run but couldn't stand on my left leg, so I started hopping but wasn't fast enough to catch up to the wagon. In a last-ditch effort, I began shouting. When my mother looked back and finally stopped, I fell to the ground. Mom ran to help me to my feet, but my leg buckled again. I didn't understand the pain. At that point, I was probably more afraid of the consequences of falling and creating this confusion.

My mom knew a lady who was a nurse and happened to live close by. The next thing I knew, she was lifting me into her pickup truck and we were off to the hospital. My leg was definitely broken; I had it X-rayed and a cast put on. For the next week, I was in the hospital learning how to walk with crutches. I met a very nice man named Andy Margitan during that hospital stay. He owned one of the largest strawberry farms in the valley. My mother used to pick for him during strawberry season.

While I was on crutches, my mother kept me at home because she didn't trust anyone near me: the slightest shove might cause me to lose my balance. This eventually did happen; my leg was broken again in the same place, so the old cast had to be removed and a new one put on. When I finally returned to school, I had tests coming out my ears. Even though I had missed a lot of work, I was promoted to the next grade.

So school was going fairly well. Other than for the two bad characters I came up against, I enjoyed my time in grade seven. I got along real fine with the other kids. But not everything was positive at home. My mother suffered humiliation over how she dealt with things as an individual and as a mother, because she had had a traditional upbringing. To have a son such as me out of wedlock went against traditional values. To make things worse, my Native ancestry was in question. It would be much, much later that I would discover my true identity.

When my mother's stepmother passed away, custom dictated that my mother, one of two children alive on her father's side, should take charge of the burial procedures and give-away. Ktunaxa tradition said that when either of the couple died, everything that person owned must be given away. (When my mother died, all her personal belongings were given away after my sisters took one thing each that they wanted.) When a man died, even the horses, furniture, and appliances were given away; the woman who was left had to start from scratch. She couldn't accept anything new for one year; everything must be secondhand.

In the case of my mother's stepmother, what should have been simple became a battle of ownership. My mother's father had built a barn that she and my father used to shelter the horses. It automatically became the property of her step-mother when her father died; so the stepmother's grand-children from her first husband assumed ownership of the barn following her death. A lot of bickering and name-calling happened. After the roof of the barn got torn off, my father settled the issue by offering some money, which the grand-children accepted.

Much later, I learned from an elder that because of direct inheritance, custom, and tradition, what took place should never have happened. Technically, my mother and my uncle were the heirs who were to receive money or property whether or not the deceased person had left a will. I also learned that the money was a peace offering to the plaintiffs and not for purchase of the barn.

I often wondered how many more times people would have to put up with that type of stupidity. From that experience, I learned that you cannot trust or respect your peers until you have received respect in return.

On several occasions, my mother and I ate lunch in the kitchen of a local restaurant.

"Why are we eating in the kitchen?" I used to ask her.

"We Indians are not allowed to eat in the main restaurant."

Hell, I was thinking it was a privilege. These people must have liked us so much, they wanted us to eat in their kitchen. In fact, we had to come in through the back door.

My mother and I entered a lot of places through the back door. When she wanted to buy groceries at the Imperial Groceteria, she would go in through the back and pass on her grocery list to a clerk, who in turn gathered the items on the list, put them into a box, and brought it to us with the bill. After my mother paid for the food, we left, again through the back door.

My parents were not allowed to enter restaurants, licensed premises, the liquor store, or other retail stores. When I was born, much of this type of discrimination was still happening. We were not even allowed to get a taxi home. In 1954 we were given permission to enter stores and cafés through the front door. A year earlier, Native children were allowed into public schools, provided they had short hair and were decently dressed. In 1962 Native people gained the right to purchase alcohol and were admitted to licensed premises, and in 1969 we regained the right to practise our beliefs.

1963—Easter Sunday Mass. I was the altar boy in this picture. I was fifteen years old.

As I was growing up, my mother would often tell me that all Natives in the world had traditions and a belief system long before the Catholic religion became part of our lives—beliefs that were practised through song, dance, and prayer. Traditional sweats formed the basis for grooming children of my age. They provided guidance and teachings, in hopes that the child would become a spiritual leader within the community. My mother participated in sweats to receive guidance in the upbringing of her children. However, her focus was not on the traditional side. She was oriented to Catholicism and went to church on Sundays. She wanted me to become a priest. Under my mother's influence, I became an altar boy and served Mass when the priest came to the church in the village. Among the pictures that hang in the Lower Kootenay Band complex, there is one that was taken by photographer

Hank Buckna after a church service. I am in that photograph as the altar boy. I served Mass when I was eleven and continued until I was seventeen.

My conditioning for manhood was nearing an end. Fast approaching was the tragic loss of my mother. Death signs were appearing either to other family members or to myself. Two signs remain with me, one of which occurred the weekend prior to her death.

While I was looking in a mirror combing my hair, my mother's face appeared. I had a funny feeling and turned around to look at her, but there was no one in sight.

The second sign happened two days before she died. She and I were in the barn feeding the horses. She called to me, "Climb up into the loft and throw down two bales."

I started climbing when, all of a sudden, two bales of hay came flying down the chute. I hollered, "What?"

My mother said, "Keep going and find out who did that."

At the top, there was nothing there except hay. "There's nothing up here, Mom!"

All she said was, "It's nothing to worry about." I believe she said that because she knew there was no explanation for what had happened.

Later in the summer, my dad told me the incidents were real. He told me it was my mother's out-of-body spiritual being warning us of her last few days on earth. The spirit within was in a state of unrest, preparing to depart from human form.

That terrible day after school, February 8, 1962, I hung around outside until it was time for supper. Mom wasn't home yet, but I knew Dad would be home from work soon. Maybe she would be with him. At about quarter after eight, the police paid a visit to my Uncle Gabe's, whose house was next door to ours. He left in the police car and returned about nine o'clock with Dad's wagon and team of horses.

He told us, "Your mom's dead. Sophie is dead. And they put your dad in jail—they suspect Sam of murder."

I crumbled. I was numb, in shock, angry—it was so intense I couldn't stand it. The pain was so powerful that I actually hurt. I broke down, crying like a little kid. Why, why, why?

After the autopsy was conducted Friday morning, the coroner reported that my mother had died of a respiratory condition, which caused her heart to stop. She died near the big bend of the Goat River before it flows into the Kootenay, about three-quarters of a mile from the black bridge. I have visited the place where she died several times.

After thirty-eight years, I still remember that day as if it were yesterday. At the age of thirteen, I was forced to understand death. I found it helpful to know about the "Happy Hunting Grounds," the "Spirit World," "Heaven," knowing I would eventually meet my mother again and be with her. I've had the opportunity for spirit travel, to be in contact with her, to hear her explain to me the reasons things turned out the way they did. I have learned to forgive and accept what life has to offer.

At the time, I didn't have the opportunity to grieve her death. I never had the chance to tell her how much I loved her. For all of those years, I have felt abandonment, and I have found that I've had to work through that grief patiently and persistently. In time, I know the hurt won't be so bad; it is all part of healing.

I've never returned to my old form. I don't believe anyone ever does, but we do have to choose between moving forward and wallowing in self-pity. I often wonder what my parents would be like today if sickness and alcohol had not taken hold of their short lives. As I reflect on all the pain and hurt I've gone through with the loss of my parents, sisters, uncles, aunties, and friends, I am stronger and healthier.

But on that sad day in February, I lost the desire for school and just about everything that life had to offer.

4

TWO WORLDS

IN THE SUMMER AFTER MY MOTHER'S PASSING, I HAD one of the most beautiful experiences that anyone could wish for. I had a vision that I shared only with my father. I knew he was going through a depression—he neglected things and didn't say much.

He woke me up early that special day to tell me I didn't have to haul hay with him because he was going with his boss to check the cattle in the Yahk area. I got up anyway, made breakfast, read a couple of comic books (*Kid Colt Outlaw* and *Rawhide Kid* were my favourites) and started a detective story about homicide. It took me a while because I'm a slow reader.

At midday I decided to chop wood and fill the bin. Later I picked up a deck of cards to play a little solitaire. I can't account for the time between two o'clock in the afternoon and nine o'clock that night when I decided to tell my story for my dad.

"When I was playing cards, I heard a voice calling me again and again. I didn't pay much attention to it. It sounded like it was coming from your bedroom. I got scared because it was Mom's voice. I hollered her name but fear swallowed me, and I said, 'Oh hell, you're dead.'

"Then she started calling me from outside. She kept calling. I headed out the back door in a trance. I could see a bright light in the doorway of the sweat lodge. Then everything went blank."

I told my dad that when I woke up, I was sitting on the ledge at The Point. There's a twenty-five foot drop, but my mother stood in front of me making sign language. I understood her message; she was telling me to be careful.

"You're growing up, son," she said. "There will be obstacles in your path, and one of them is alcohol. It will challenge you and will always be in front of you. If you indulge to the extreme, you will not live long. It is said you will help your people for a long time. If you choose the right path, you will be given guidance to this end and your people will be happy for you, they will have nice homes and a school to teach their young, money in their pockets, and good, healthy lives."

Dad sat patiently and listened. When I finished, he said, "That message was from the Great Spirit. It came in the form of your mother because you are still missing her. The Great Spirit works in many ways to protect and guide the people, and you are special. You must try to carry out the message."

At that critical point in my life, in the five years between the death of my mother and the death of my father, all spiritual teachings became unimportant to me. In grade eight, I found that school became very demanding, girlfriends needed attention, homework had to be done. There were chores at home, but I wanted to stay after school for extracurricular activities such as basketball and track and field. Life was definitely changing. All of a sudden, my time was no longer mine.

As with a lot of teenagers, alcohol became a way of life. Band members were constantly indulging, and it was easy for me and my friends to get hold of booze, usually beer or wine. Sometimes we would get the older men to get the liquor for us through their bootleggers, or we would wait until people got drunk and then help ourselves. Often we would drink just so much out of the bottles and add water to make up what we drank.

However, I managed all right with good teachers and good marks. I made the basketball team but didn't stick it out. I made the track team too; my fastest recorded times for the mile were 4:58 and 5:05. But I couldn't show my stuff because I twisted my ankle at the time of the meet. Today my left ankle still twists as if I were double-jointed.

Two nights a week were dedicated to boxing practice. My father didn't really agree with the sport, but he supported me anyway. Once I got the hang of it, there wasn't anyone I couldn't box with. I had a super left hook (I'm left-handed) and a smooth overhand right that could jar an opponent to the point of knocking him out. There were times my fights were very close, and other times I thought I was robbed of the nod.

My coach in Creston, Mike Moore, made a champion out of me. I remember boxing in the old Civic Centre for the East/West Lightweight (132 pounds) Championship one

Blossom Festival weekend. I almost knocked my opponent out in the first round, but we were only fighting two-minute rounds for three rounds. I won by unanimous decision, although my competitor, Ron White, was a game fighter. When I later ran across him in Vernon, he told me, "Chris, you just about had me!" His coach had been Herb Stanton, who was well-respected by all the coaches from the East and West Kootenays as well as those in Sandpoint, Coeur d'Alene, and Kellogg (in Idaho), Polson (in Montana), and Spokane, Washington.

Mike Moore moved to Cranbrook when he was offered steadier employment with a roofing company, and he worked until he became a paraplegic as a result of falling off a roof. Shortly after, many of the boxers he had trained threw a surprise birthday party for him. He wept as he read the message in the birthday card, which we had all signed. It was an emotional moment for all of us.

The Creston Boxing Club went on many trips—Calgary, Spokane, Polson, to name a few. The club hosted boxing cards in Bonners Ferry, Idaho, which was where I met Tom Lafaye and his brother, Richard. I used to hitchhike to Bonners for boxing practice twice a week after the Creston club folded. Tom was one of the coaches. I would meet him in a surprise encounter in a movie theatre several years later in Longview, Oregon, where he was working at the time.

I think fondly of those boxing memories. I still work out to stay in shape, practising both left- and right-hand jabs.

1962—This was a "let's get together for a group picture" party. Joe Pierre, Robert Louie, me, Steve Pierre behind the straw hat, Adrian Louie and Florine Louie.

My friend Adrian Louie was an excellent boxer. Before he got sick, he was very athletic, also good at playing ball and hockey. After his eighteenth birthday, he was confined to a wheelchair when a spinal infection left him paralyzed on his left side. He was flown to Sardis, B.C., where he remained in hospital for about three years. On one visit home, they flew him to Cranbrook and transported him by car to Creston and the village. The people had a big welcome party for him, with hot dogs, corn on the cob, marshmallows, and Kool-aid.

When it was time for him to return to Sardis, it was a sad moment for us. We didn't know when he would be home the next time. I really took it hard, and I went along with his family to see him off at the Cranbrook airport, which, at that time, was located in the industrial area just west of the railway tracks. Adrian's mother and sister and I waved goodbye to him as the stewardess wheeled him to the plane. Both Isobel and Irene were crying; I couldn't help myself and started crying, too. It was one of the saddest trips I've ever made.

Every fall, I enjoyed getting home from school and heading off to hunt for *tanqu¢* (grouse). I became a good shot with the .22-calibre rifle. I considered myself a very skillful sniper, bagging one or two grouse at a time.

Learning how to hunt was a big part of my traditional life. My father would set me out at the edge of a clearing and ask, "How would you get to the middle of the field without being seen? What direction would you go if there was a deer standing there?" He taught me to take into account the wind factor, noise level, and ground cover.

Before my fourteenth birthday, I shot my first deer. I was proud of myself. Dad told me that I had to give it away, and my reaction was "What for?"

"It's traditional. When you shoot your first deer or elk, you must give it away except for the heart. The heart you cook up and eat with your family. That way, you are ensuring yourself good luck in future hunts."

Every morning during hunting season, I would walk to the top of the hill, all the way along to the west side of the present airport and north of Fox Tree Hill. One day in November during *Tanukɬuk ¢upqa* (deer-rutting season), I happened upon three deer. Two of them ran, a buck and a doe, so there was just one doe standing broadside of me, probably fifty yards straight across the ravine. It seemed that deer was daring me to shoot.

I slowly raised the rifle and pointed towards it, right in behind the shoulders. Bang! It went down, got back up, and ran directly north. I knew they always ran in a circle and usually ended up about where they got spooked or shot. So I travelled in a semi-circle, west and then north. I stopped every once in a while, listening for brush breaking or heavy breathing, checking the wind for smell coming my way.

After an hour, I decided I'd have to pick up the blood trail if there was one. I walked back to the exact spot where the deer had stood. There was a bit of blood on the ground where it fell, so I followed the hoof tracks and the blood. The deer had gone north for about thirty yards and directly east for another hundred yards, then north again for twenty yards, west for about one hundred and fifty, and finally headed south to within one hundred yards of where I shot it.

The deer was lying under a stand of small evergreens. It must have died a couple of hours earlier because it was nearing eleven a.m., and I knew that when I was getting close to the hill it had been shortly after eight-thirty. I turned the doe over and faced it west, cut its throat, bled it, and gutted it. I kept the heart—what was left of it—and the liver. I placed the spleen on a branch facing east and said a prayer thanking the Creator for this successful hunt and for future hunts.

I tried packing the deer, but it was too heavy, so I dragged it all the way down to the bank of Highway 21. By this time, it was around two or three in the afternoon and it had started to drizzle, a light rain. When I got home, Dad still wasn't back from work, so I dragged the animal next to the highway so it would be easy to load into the wagon.

When we finally got the deer home, I finished skinning it, and we quartered it. Dad asked, "Was this one with any other deer?"

"*Hiy*, there was another doe and they were with a buck."

"Funny that the doe was with the other two because she's a dry doe, and they usually get singled out of the herd." How he knew to say that, I'll never know.

During the summer, when school was finished, I didn't hang around home much. I packed my little suitcase to stay with the Louies at Nicks Island on Indian Reserve No. 4. The whole Louie family was there, except for the three who were at the Coqualeetza Hospital in Sardis being treated for tuberculosis. Robert Louie had been my friend since I was six. My mother and I would drive out frequently to visit the family. When I first met Robert, he was pulling a little red wagon up to the top of the dyke and riding down the hill past the house. That first day we rode the wagon for a while and then walked the trail to the Kootenay River, where we undressed and jumped into the water, swimming and mud-crawling around. Later we had a lunch of tripe and fried bread that his mother and grandmother made. Robert and I ate the stuff like there was no tomorrow.

There was only one problem with living out on the flats— access to stores, television, and other people was non-existent. However, we still managed to have a great time that summer. I continued to fish, hunt, and canoe the Kootenay

River, enjoying life as it should be enjoyed. I even earned $20 on a five-day job hauling and stacking baled hay for Mr. E. Fry and his son, David, who were renting the alfalfa field from the Band.

I have a vivid memory of being harassed constantly by a large bear, which was no ordinary bear, but a grizzly. We were pretty safe during the day, but at night the bear would prowl around the cabin, upsetting things and several times slapping the dogs, knocking them back as if to say "Shut up!" because they were yapping fiercely. The trauma continued for four days before Grandma Marianne Ernest decided she was going to walk the bear out of the area, which she did. In the spirit world, when one inherits a grizzly bear as a guide, the spirit wanders, taking natural form to find someone to put it out of its misery. Grandma Marianne didn't want the responsibility, which is why she led the bear away. The rest of the summer, we were spiritually harassed from dusk until dawn by this grizzly.

When I returned home in August of 1963, Dad wanted to sit down with me and discuss the future, but I certainly wasn't prepared to hear what he had to say. I listened, and I did not like what he was telling me. I was feeling neglected and unwanted.

"It's real nice that you had the summer with the Louies, Chris. Being alone without you and Doreen and Rudy gave me a lot of time to think." He said he was still mourning my mother, and that he needed more time to himself.

"Have you ever thought of going to school in Cranbrook?" he asked me. "I want you to consider going to room and board at St. Eugene's Mission School. You have to make the choice yourself."

And so I did. I attended Mt. Baker High School in Cranbrook, not because I wanted to, but out of consideration for Dad. Doreen followed shortly after, and she remained there for three years.

The principal at St. Eugene's, Father LaPlante, and Brother MacDonald met me when I arrived. Brother MacDonald escorted me to the boys' side of the school. He asked if I had eaten supper, and I said no. We went on to the storage room on the third floor. "You'll have to get rid of the clothes you have on," he told me. He handed me all the things I would need: bed sheets, pillowcase, blankets, towels, toothpaste and toothbrush, a comb, and clothing, including pajamas. He led me into a huge room, a classroom in size, but full of beds. He told me to choose a bed and helped me to make it. Before he left, he explained there would be an inspection every morning and that we were to keep our room and beds tidy. I went to bed without supper.

In the morning, Brother MacDonald stuck his head into the washroom and said, "By the way, Mr. Luke, we pray around here, and Mass is at seven o'clock in the morning in the chapel. I expect you to join the boys."

I went back to the dorm and sat on the edge of my new bed. I sat for a long time, feeling the same loneliness I felt when my mother passed away. I wanted to leave but knew it wouldn't be a good idea because my father would only say, "You didn't give it a chance."

The beds on either side of me were occupied by Peter Birdstone who was from the nearby St. Mary's Reserve, and David George from the Osoyoos Band in Oliver. Both of them were also attending high school in Cranbrook. I made friends with them right away. They told me the rules didn't really apply to seniors who were only boarding there, and I felt a lot better knowing it wouldn't be as strict as I thought.

I didn't mind all the praying we did, but I started having problems with the school work and was falling behind in algebra and science. My grades were not what I expected. I soon became frustrated, lonesome, and afraid of failure. I didn't get the help I needed to get better marks, and the food at the residential school wasn't all that great. The discipline was the last straw.

One weekend in November, Peter and I wanted to have some fun and to find some of the wild parties that were supposed to be happening on the St. Mary's Reserve. We decided to sneak out of the dormitory and made our getaway out the north exit door, using the fire escape stairway. We had trouble finding a party, but we did come across a pickup truck with people Peter knew. They had wine and offered each of us a big gulp. The more wine we drank, the braver we got. It was about four in the morning before we made our way back to the school. Our beds were still the same way we had left them— stuffed with pillows to look like we were sleeping.

No sooner were we asleep than Brother MacDonald was ringing the morning bell and tapping at our beds to get us up for Sunday church in the school chapel. I was feeling pretty sick because I had drunk too much and hadn't had any sleep. The day went by slowly; no one said anything to me or to Peter. We spent a good deal of time outside, mainly because we felt so lousy. We told each other, "Boy, we got away with it this time." Later in the afternoon, Peter took off for home. Unfortunately, during study hour, Father LaPlante called me to the front of the classroom. Somehow, he had found out about our night out. He began by describing my behaviour in a derogatory manner and ordered me to extend my hands. He gave me ten lashes on each one. Later my hands felt like clubs, swollen as if I was wearing a pair of rubber gloves with air in them. To add insult to injury, I was made to kneel in front of all the girls in the cafeteria, my tray of food on the floor in front of me. I was expected to eat off that tray.

But I didn't do it. I disappointed Father LaPlante and Brother MacDonald and all the people who were waiting for me to eat off the floor. I said I wasn't a dog. The girls were giggling; I wondered if they felt sorry for me or embarrassed for me. "Aren't you going to eat?" Brother MacDonald asked. "Snakes in the grass usually eat."

"Not this snake," I said. I felt angry and humiliated; I felt I had served my penance by being strapped. I was not the person they were describing as a drunk, a failure who wouldn't amount to anything. I was not going to allow it to happen again if I could help it. Absolutely no way was that school going to break my spirit.

Peter dropped out just after New Year's. My marks didn't improve, but I held on until the end of February, when I was homeward bound on a snowy morning. Hitchhiking, it took me most of the day to get to Creston from Cranbrook. My first ride, a pickup truck, took me only as far as the Hiawatha gas station. Second was a grader operator, who was plowing. He let me off near Moyie Lake and after an hour or so of walking along the highway between three-foot-high snowbanks, I had a ride all the way back to Creston.

I got out at Anderson's Drugstore, headed west past Creston Builders, across the railway tracks, past Turnbull's secondhand store, and straight south. It was dark, but I didn't really care because I was in familiar territory. I took my time walking and stopped to visit my sister, Pauline, who lived on Highway 21 between the turnoff to Goat River Bottom and the Lower Kootenay community.

"I'm here for good," I told her. "I'm not going back to school in Cranbrook."

"Well, it's your life. I don't know what Dad is going to say about you running away from school."

"I'll worry about Dad when I get home."

I also stopped to say hello to my friend, Robert. When I told him I was home to stay, he nodded in approval.

At my house, my sister Mary confronted me. She had moved in to watch over Rudy, my younger brother, while he went back to school. "What are you doing here?"

My dad, who was giving Rudy a haircut, came next. "What's going on? Why are you home?" Talk about being bombarded with questions.

"I'm not doing so good at school. If I don't pick up on my marks, I have to leave anyway." I told him about the food and the discipline and the incident with the priest and the principal.

"You should have told me about that at Christmas."

"If I did, what would you have done?"

"I would have let you stay home. Are you going back to school here?" he asked.

"Big question, Dad…I was thinking that I'll just go back in the fall."

"Fine, just do it."

Boy, what a relief that was! I believe that was one of the first times that my father agreed without allowing his own feelings to decide the outcome of our discussion.

I spent the spring and summer doing odd jobs like chopping wood, pruning and thinning apples, mending fences, and helping with the haying. We'd load it, haul it, and stack it in several areas on the reservation, because my father rotated the herd of cattle from one area to the next.

He did keep mentioning to me the need to get an education—it was important for survival. No matter what the circumstances, he said, there would always be issues that would pop up and need immediate solving.

5

LOVE AND RULES

THAT FALL I STARTED SCHOOL AGAIN AT PRINCE CHARLES Secondary to repeat grade nine. My home room was the art room, which was a treat because I loved to draw—animals, cars, and sometimes people's faces. I got A on every assignment. Today, I don't care to draw or paint, but I do have an eye for detail, and that's what I look for in other people's art.

During that school year, 1964-65, I began to use Luke as my last name. Previously, because of my particular situation, I was registered with my mother's last name (she was Sophie Sam), but I also had my adopted father's last name, Luke, which was registered with the Department of Indian Affairs in Ottawa. So I was Chris Sam to my friends, who were surprised when I started calling myself Christopher Sam Luke. They thought maybe my mother had remarried.

School was somewhat interesting. I enjoyed math. Two of the class wizards would have contests to see who was quicker with the answers. Because of them, I learned my multiplication tables. English was not one of my stronger subjects, but I did enjoy the stories the teacher, Mr. William Betcher, shared

Yaqan Nukiy Village, south side in 1962. The photo was taken from the church steeple. The band hall is in the foreground and our home (Lukes) is third from the hall.

with us. One assignment was to write a book report on a true story. I chose one about the war and Adolf Hitler and how he had died. I only read half the book and had one page written by the time the report was due. Because I hadn't finished, I was instructed to give my report orally. I am not a comedian and it was the first time that I ever got up in front of a class, but I had everyone laughing. I believe it was the language I was using, like "kicked the bucket" instead of "died." As it turned out, I failed English, which meant I would have to repeat grade nine. I also failed science.

Again in January, I quit. I worked with Dad during the rest of that school year, promising that I'd return in the fall of 1965.

The first day of the school year 1965-66 was a nightmare. I had to face some ridicule. They were asking why I thought I could do it this time. My confidence shattered, I told my counsellor I would pack it in if I didn't do well before Christmas.

But something else decided it for me. One morning I was building a fire in the cook stove and was too lazy to chop kindling. I got out the kerosene, poured it on several pieces of wood in the stove, and blew on it. It exploded in my face, burning my hair, my eyebrows, and almost blinding me. Sure enough, before school had barely started, I took the easy way out again, quit, and made no more promises to my dad.

Early in the spring the Indian Affairs education worker, who seldom travelled out of the district office in Kamloops, came to see me, particularly to find out why I had dropped out of school once again.

I gave Peter all my reasons and said, "I'd be happy to go to school somewhere else, where there's no pressures."

"Would you be willing to go to the Kelowna Vocational Technical School, VTS, if I made the arrangements?"

"Yes, I would."

"I'll be back in September to see if you still feel the same way," he said.

I didn't mention this to anyone, not even Dad. He had me

working with him in the fields loading, hauling, and stacking hay. The fun part was unloading the trailer by placing the baled hay onto an elevator inside the hay shed. I had at least three, sometimes four, bales on the elevator heading up into the stack. Dad would holler at me to slow down every once in a while from the top of the stack.

That summer of 1966 I got serious about a girl, Brenda, whom I met while swimming in the Goat River. She was a very special person—loveable, humorous, and caring. She had a deep understanding. Every chance I had when not working, I would meet her. We did a lot together—walked, hiked, swam, went horseback riding. We saw a lot of movies, took in some teen dances, and simply enjoyed each other's company.

One day, my dad told me he needed me to drive tractor and pick up the balance of the baled hay in the field.

"How many bales?" I asked.

"Probably about two hundred and fifty."

"I'll do it tomorrow."

"Sure."

Tomorrow came and I said, "I'm not feeling too well. I'm sick."

"Okay," said Dad. "Stay in bed."

Actually, Brenda and I had already made plans for the day. I met her at the black bridge, as it was called then. We went for a dip and decided to hike down to the Kootenay River at the mouth of the Goat. It was several hours later that we walked back up to the bridge. We took our last dip and began to say our goodbyes, but we were unable to walk in opposite directions. Brenda decided to walk with me partway home. We headed south to the white bridge and stood near the middle of it overlooking the river, talking about her parents and other people in general.

Just then we heard the clip-clop of a horse crossing the bridge. We looked up to see my father on his way home. "Hi," he said, and pointed at me. "I'll see you at home."

I knew immediately that meant he wanted to talk to me. Once he was in the distance, I said to Brenda, "My dad's pissed off. I know it."

"Why would he be? He seemed friendly, and he said hi to me, too."

"Well, that's just it—he's not pissed off at you, but me. He wanted me to work with him today, and I told him I was sick, and here I am with you. I guess I should get home before trouble catches up to me."

I took off in a slow jog and picked up the pace as I approached the boundaries of the reservation. Dad was sitting at the table eating supper, so I joined him. When we finished eating, he started talking about how relationships of mixed cultural backgrounds never work out.

"I don't want you getting mixed up with a white girl or white women, because they don't understand us. They don't try to understand. White people are dictators and do things to satisfy themselves. They only care about themselves.

"Your mother and I were brought together by our families. I spent half a year with her family hunting, trapping, doing all the things a man is supposed to do to gain respect and earn the right to marry a woman. Your mother did the same—cooked, cleaned, and took care of my family. She did the things a woman does to earn her way with a man."

This custom of living with each other and the families is probably the main reason there are not many marriage breakups among Native couples.

My father told me a woman cannot have eye contact with a man until she gets married and cannot speak to any man unless he speaks to her. "After a man or woman dies, the person still living cannot have any kind of relationship with the opposite sex for one year and cannot marry for three years. If your mother had a sister who was single, I would have to marry her after the third year. That is the tradition."

I remember thinking it's tough to be an Indian. I wondered why people were not practising these customs if they were so important. I'm glad that everything is changing. When I view relationships today, I see it's the individuals who either make or break the union—not necessarily problems with cultural background, although it can be a hindrance if there is lack of understanding.

My dad went on with his lecture. "From the time you were born, you have received some gifts, and they will slowly become part of your life. That includes the person you are supposed to marry…When the time is right, you will meet the lady who will be with you for the rest of your life."

Big deal, this guy's not getting married, I said to myself, all the while wondering who I was supposed to marry, where I was going to live, how many children we would have, what kind of job I would be doing.

I worked hard that summer and saved up all the money I

earned. I even went fighting fire, which helped a lot in purchasing clothes that I knew I would need.

Summer was soon gone. One fall evening Dad came home from work and told me that Bob Comfort wanted me to haul hay for him. My father worked for Bob before he went to work for George Hood, so their acquaintance with one another was one of mutual respect.

The very next day, I rode with Dad to Comforts' driveway. I knocked three times on the back door and Mrs. Comfort greeted me. I told her I was ready for work. Bob offered me a cup of coffee.

Soon we were in his three-ton truck heading towards the West Creston ferry landing. About a quarter of a mile from the main highway, we turned left into a hay field. Sitting there was a big pile of hay, a stack eighty feet long and thirty feet wide and about twelve feet high. Talk about a lot of bales! The objective of the whole exercise was to move the stack into the barn next to Bob's house.

I threw the bales and Bob stacked. It took us forty-five minutes to an hour to load the truck. To unload took about the same amount of time. We managed three truckloads that day.

After work I waited for Dad to meet me at the junction of Comforts' driveway and Highway 21. He was the only community member left on the reserve who still had a horse and wagon to use as a means of transportation. Before long, I heard the horses trotting down the highway. As they approached, I could see that Dad had a slight grin on his face.

"How was your day?"

"It turned out all right," I said, jumping into the wagon. "For an old guy and a young guy, we managed three loads on that big truck."

My father was pleased. "Bob's always been a hard worker at whatever he does…Did you have lunch?"

"Yeah! Roast beef and mashed potatoes and vegetables. They asked me if I wanted to stay for supper, too, but I said no." We went on down the highway, enjoying the last of the sunshine. Then I threw a left curve at him. "Why haven't you got married again?"

"I don't know. The right woman hasn't come along yet."

"How can a person know that a certain woman is the right one?"

"Remember what I told you about gifts," he said. "It's a gift to know who is the right woman for yourself."

There was no more said as we got closer to home.

I kept right on working for Bob Comfort. The second stand of alfalfa was ready to be cut. I guess I spent at least three whole weeks working for him. I spent whatever free time I had swimming and catching the Indian summer weather we were having.

Not all my jobs were as positive as working for the Comforts. I remember Dad getting very angry when I told him how I was treated on one job. Robert and I were hired by a guy to herd his cattle from the Lower Kootenay wetlands to his property in Erickson on Stocks-Jackson Road. We herded the cattle all day with no lunch, no water, no nothing. When we finally got the cattle home, I thought the guy might at least offer us some dinner. We could smell the sausages cooking! But it didn't happen. We were told, "Thanks, boys. I'll have some money ready for you on Monday."

So we walked home and were so tired we didn't even bother to eat. When Monday rolled around, we went back for our pay. We kept going back for a whole week. The excuse was always, "I still haven't gone to the bank to get the money for you boys."

My dad was ready to give this man a piece of his mind. Dad was big and very strong; he could have eaten this guy for breakfast anytime he wanted to. But Robert and I have not been paid yet for that long, hard day of work.

One of the days at Comforts, Bob and I hauled in a load later than usual. It must have been the middle of the week, probably Wednesday.

"Chris, you'd better stay and have dinner with us tonight."

"Okay, I will."

During the meal, Bob said, "I heard, Chris, that you're going with the neighbour's daughter. Is that true?"

"Yes, it is."

"How does your dad feel about that?"

"He doesn't like it, but there's really not too much he can do about it."

"What about the girl's father? What does he think?"

"I haven't really had the opportunity to talk to him, so I don't know what to say about that."

"Well, Chris, I hope everything works out for you."

When we finished eating, I asked to use the phone and called Brenda to see if she wanted to talk or go for a walk. I told her where I was, and she said she would meet me halfway. At about nine o'clock we met, hugged and kissed, and then headed for her place. It was about nine o'clock.

"Dad's not home," she said, "so we can talk for a little while."

I told her about my plan to go to school in the Okanagan. She really didn't like the idea, but she knew it was going to happen anyway.

"I should get on home. It's getting late, and you should be in bed by now."

"Yeah, I should be, but I'm not going to."

"Well, I'm going home. I don't want to be here when your mom and dad come back."

We embraced again and I left. I was near the corner of Canyon Street and Highway 21 when Brenda came running.

"You just can't leave like that!"

"What about your mom and dad?"

"I told my brother to say I just went out for a walk."

We started walking south towards the reserve. I asked, "What has your father said about us going together?"

"He doesn't like it, but that doesn't mean that he dislikes you as a person."

"How do you know that? Did he say that?"

"No."

"See, you don't know."

By this time, we were kind of arguing but nothing serious—asking each other questions to see how our parents' beliefs affected our relationship. We were near the section of the

Erickson back road known as Archibald Hill when a vehicle came heading in our direction. It was a dark blue pickup truck.

Brenda said, "Oh! It's Dad."

Her father was a proud, hard-working kind of guy. Much of the time he was a loner and expressed himself in a "my way or no way at all" attitude.

I was feeling nervous. What was going to happen? The pickup stopped and her dad said, "Get in."

She opened the door and asked, "Can you give Chris a lift home?"

"No," her father said. Brenda got in and he turned the truck around and headed in the direction he came from.

I expected his answer, but I thought it was rude, and I felt hurt because I hadn't asked Brenda to walk that far. No, he certainly didn't care for me or for the relationship I had with his daughter. Because of that little incident, Brenda was grounded for the next two weeks. She definitely could not see me or talk to me at any time. So I stayed away, but checking the mail I found two letters that she had written while in school. She expressed how much she missed me and how stupid it was for her to think that her dad would never come after her like he did.

On the other hand, Brenda's mother was more understanding; she gave me rides home whenever she could, and I certainly appreciated that. She liked the idea of my returning to school in Kelowna. She said my education was very important, that I was going to need that education to remain a survivor in this world. She said so many changes were taking place and that we had to fit in somewhere.

The two weeks seemed long, but finally Brenda and I were dating again and visiting one another on weekends. Her father seemed to soften up, and he began talking to me. I think he realized that Brenda and I cared for each other and weren't about to let him sabotage our friendship.

Near the end of September, I received another visit from the education worker. He asked about my decision to return to school.

"I haven't changed my mind…Did you find me a place in Kelowna?"

"Yes, you start the day after New Year's, and you'll be room and boarding with an elderly couple, the Lunts. They live on Ethel Street, about six blocks from the technical school. One other thing, Chris, you won't be alone. Do you know Jerry Gregoire?"

The name rang a bell. "Yes, I remember a kid at the residential school in Cranbrook."

"Well," said Peter, "Jerry remembers you and he's looking forward to sharing a room and going to school with you."

"Great! I won't feel alone."

"I'll try to stay in touch with you. Here's my card. If anything comes up before you're supposed to leave, phone me collect. I'll let them know you'll be phoning in an emergency situation. I'll send your travel voucher about three weeks before you leave."

I waved to Peter as he drove away. I had a joyous yet sad feeling. What was I getting myself into? Did I really want to leave home? I decided it was time to tell Dad what I was doing.

Dad and I took turns cooking and it was my turn, so I whipped up some potatoes, green beans, and deer meat. As soon as he had put the horses away and washed up, I told him my plans.

"Dad, I have something to tell you. Remember, when the Indian agent came around last spring?"

"*Hiy.*"

"He wanted to know if I wanted to continue my education and I said yes. He came back today and I'm planning to go to school in Kelowna."

"Good! Now sit down and listen to me. You have tried school for the last three years, and you have quit each time. I hope for your sake, for your dead mother's sake, and for me that you're going to stick it out this time, no matter how hard it may seem or how lonesome you may get. Let me be proud of you this time. If you get lonesome, just write and I'll get Mary or Pauline to write for me, and it will be just like I'm right there with you."

We sat in silence for a few minutes.

"Not this time, Dad. Not this time. I promise I'll stick it out and I know I'll do well."

With all the work I'd had, I managed to save up just over $300 that I spent on clothing. I even bought myself a suitcase, which I still have today.

My dad saw all that I had bought and said, "Your heart is in a good place. You've taken the first steps and now are heading in the right direction."

1966—This was the day the community buried my father. Father Morelli presided. I had the honour of carrying my father's cross from our house to the church and up to the Yaqan Nukiy Cemetery.

6

GOODBYES

THE BITTER WEATHER OF NOVEMBER WAS SETTING IN, and it began to rain a lot. Sometimes *Katitu* (my father), didn't go to work because he was nursing a cold. Mary watched over him and did most of the cooking.

Dad didn't improve. It seemed that the cold had settled into his chest. Both Mary and I told him that he should see the doctor, but he refused to go. He kept telling us that he would get better. We kept the fire going so the house was always nice and warm. We put a pot of water on the stove to generate moisture to help Dad get over his cold.

Although he seemed to get better, he admitted he was feeling a bit weak, so we told him to stay in bed. I phoned Dempsey Hood to explain that Dad was very sick and wouldn't be able to go to work for at least another week. "Well," said Dempsey, "tell Sam to get a lot of rest and get better before coming back." Dad just smiled when I told him.

On November 22, Thursday, I heard Dad shuffling around having breakfast. I got up and joined him; we ate porridge and toast.

"I'm going to try to go to work today," he said.

"Are you feeling better?"

"Not too bad…I'm going to work."

He wasn't sounding very good to me; he sounded all congested inside. I watched him walk his horse to the shed. As he was cinching the saddle, he staggered. All his movements were unsteady. I knew then that he wasn't strong enough to go to work.

"Dad, maybe you're not ready to go anywhere right now. You need more rest."

He didn't pay any attention to me, just went right on doing his thing, getting ready to leave. He walked to the left side of the horse and made an attempt to get on, but he was just too weak. On his second attempt, I gave him a boost from the rear, and he fell completely over the other side. He lay on the ground for several minutes.

"Help me up."

"You'd better get back into the house."

With my help, he got settled into bed. I put the horse away, watered him, and left feed in the stall. I wondered what Dad would say if I called the ambulance to take him to the hospital. He probably wouldn't think too much of me.

It was around ten o'clock when Dad called for some water. I could hear him coughing, almost choking. As I brought him the water, he took a last breath of air, and then silence.

I stood with the dipper of water, shocked. I didn't know what to do.

Finally, I was able to holler, "Daaaad! Mary…Dad's dead! He's dead…He just died."

I threw the dipper into the sink. I was so stunned I didn't

A sad day—
This is me on
November 25,
1966. We had
just buried my
father.

know what to do except to run out of the house. Zachary Basil happened to be walking by, and I told him about Dad. He took off in the direction of the church and rang the bell. Within a few minutes, everyone in the village had the bad news. It didn't take too long for the police and ambulance to arrive at our house. The police questioned me and took pictures and told the ambulance attendants to move my dad's body.

It was Friday evening when they brought him back to the house for the wake. Thinking of my mother, and being now aware of what death meant, I dreaded going through another funeral. But it had been my father who taught me about acceptance and life after death.

Doreen came home from Cranbrook, and I told her everything that had happened with Dad during the time he was sick. She cried for the longest time. My brother, Rudy, was probably the most devastated by the loss. I remember when he came home from school and heard that Dad was dead. "No way," he said, "I just saw him with Sam Ignatius and Clara in the wagon."

I told him again, but he didn't believe it. When Sam and Clara got home, there sitting in the back of the wagon was Lazarus Louie. That's when it must have dawned on Rudy, because he hollered out, "Daddy! Daddy! Where's my daddy?" It took us a long time to settle Rudy down.

During the wake, Doreen and I said the rosary together— probably the one and only time I said the rosary in its entirety. Today, I still don't say it; I don't have the feel for it. I had the honour of saying a few words about Dad and the privilege of carrying his cross from the house to the church and, after, up to the community graveyard. It was very sad, especially during the lowering of the casket, when people sang in Ktunaxa for the Creator to accept the body of the deceased back into the ground, to release the spirit of the departed to the home of the Creator, known to us as the happy hunting ground.

Following the burial, I was told that I had a position to fulfill within the community: I was to take care of the graves, just as Dad and Uncle Gabe did. Today, Rudy and I still make these preparations unless the immediate family decides otherwise.

When I lost my father, I was seventeen and Zach Basil was in his mid-thirties. His words to me then about life and purpose and the Creator remained in my mind and heart, powerful words about the reasons behind Dad's death and my responsibility within the family. He said others in my family would be looking to me for direction now that I was head of the household.

The very next week I received in the mail the travel voucher I had been waiting for. Doreen was ready to return to Cranbrook for school after spending an extra week at home.

"I'll probably still be here when you come for the Christmas holidays," I told her.

She seemed happy about that. "You'd better be here when I get back! Don't leave without saying goodbye."

I spent the rest of my time hiking and hunting along the hills towards the border. On weekends, I would visit with Brenda; sometimes we took in a movie or a dance, but mostly we just went for walks.

The Christmas season was fast approaching, and I started making plans for the day I was going to leave. I thought I should wait for Doreen and leave the day before New Year's. I walked to town, taking the voucher with me to buy my one-way ticket to Kelowna. I was somewhat excited about the whole thing.

About a month after my dad's death, Yakan Nukiy experienced another tragedy in which a house fire took the life of a band member. There was a lot of controversy in the village over the incident. Foul play was suspected and I learned much later that the speculation proved to be factual. The suspect was charged with arson and manslaughter and served eighteen months in an institution in the Lower Mainland.

The night of the fire, Brenda and I had gone to the teen dance at the Legion hall. On the way home, I had a spiritual experience that I'll never forget. As I rounded the corner before the approach to the village, on the left-hand side of Frank Basil's driveway, I saw a guy standing in what I thought was at least a foot of snow. I couldn't see his face, but for some reason I knew who it was, so I yelled out, "You should get back up to the house!" It was cold out and I didn't want him coming onto the highway where he could get run over. I glanced down and noticed he wasn't standing in the snow, but above it.

A shiver gripped me, and I turned away immediately. When I glanced back, the figure was gone. I took off at a run and didn't look back again. I had noticed the sky was well lit up. Now I knew there was a fire, probably a house fire. As I approached, I knew whose house was burning. There was no one around except for one policeman sitting in his patrol car. He called me over.

"Where did you just come from?" he asked.

"From a dance in town."

"Did you see anyone on the road on your way home?"

"No, I didn't see anyone…What happened?"

"Someone lit the house on fire. Someone was inside."

I knew then what I had seen a few minutes before. I knew it was connected to the fire. I was hoping whoever was burned didn't suffer much. I went home to bed and slept until Mary woke me up.

"Thomas White's house burned down, and Louis burned in it," she said.

"What did you say?"

"Louis Basil burned up in Thomas's house."

I sat right up in bed. "You know, I saw Louis's ghost last night standing by the side of the driveway up to Frank's place."

"Well, you got spooked," Mary said. "Louis's ghost was just saying goodbye, or maybe checking to take someone with him. Who knows?"

I didn't waste any time. I got dressed and headed across to what was left of Thomas's house. The area was ribboned off and two policemen were questioning Joe Pierre and Pete White. When the interrogation was finished, I stood with Joe and Pete and Joe's uncle, Tony Pierre, to watch two men in asbestos suits rake through the ashes. Carefully, they placed what seemed to be the remains of a body into a plastic bag. Louis Basil was only thirty-four. I felt sorry, thinking about his wife Mary, his three children, about how they were going to take the loss, and about my own father and my own loss a month earlier.

Joe said, "I can't take this anymore." He turned and went back to the house next door.

I walked home across the village to tell my sister, "Yes, it's Louis. He's dead. Joe and Pete tried to save him last night. The doors were locked, but they broke a window and tried to climb through. They couldn't get in. It was too hot!"

She looked at me. "Is it true who did it?"

"According to what the police asked and the answers they got, yes, it's true."

"How could anyone be so careless?"

I answered in a joking manner, "Search me...The cops will get to the bottom of this."

Mary went right on cooking breakfast.

"Friday nights never seem to go by without someone getting hurt, someone fighting, or someone spending the night in jail," I said.

"*Hiy*, that's the way it goes around here."

We ate breakfast feeling uptight because of all that had happened during the night.

"I'm leaving tomorrow. I start school on Tuesday and I'll be spending New Year's with the Lunts in Kelowna."

"Are you ready to go?" she asked finally. "Are all your clothes washed?"

"Yes, I'm ready. I'm staying at Brenda's tonight. My bus leaves at six-thirty in the morning."

I packed my suitcase and decided to say my goodbyes to the Louie family—Rob, Wayne, Florine, Irene, Adrian, Joan, and their mom, Isobel. I also went to see Isaac (Ike) Basil, Aunt Nancy, and my sister Cecile, who was called Cisco. I crossed the village to say goodbye to Pete and the Pierres—Joe, Tony, and Steve.

I said goodbye to Mary, Rudy, little Josie, and Uncle David. Between three and four in the afternoon, I picked up my suitcase and headed out the door. It would take me at least a half hour to get to Brenda's house. I had been invited to dinner with her family, so I had to clock myself.

She mentioned the house fire. "Did someone die in it?"

"Yeah, it happened."

"Who was it?"

"You don't know him...He used to be chief. I don't want to talk about it," I said. "I'll miss you."

"I'll miss you more."

"I'm going to miss everything we did together. I'm going to miss home, hunting, taking hikes, visiting with people."

Christmas had been the only other time I'd had a meal with Brenda's family. We'd eaten turkey dinner and exchanged gifts. I remember buying a nice knitted sweater for her, and she got me Old Spice after-shave lotion and a soap set for my travelling bag.

On the night before I left for Kelowna, Brenda slipped in the question to her mom and dad.

"Maybe I can visit with Chris during the Easter break?"

Her father was in good spirits. He had told me he thought it was good that I was leaving to complete my education away from the community. He said I was allowing myself the chance to do something for my future. I was thinking he was being nice because he wouldn't have to worry about his daughter since I would be out of town.

Nevertheless, I was floored when he said, "We'll see when the time comes, and if his boarding-home parents will have you for a couple of days."

After dinner, Brenda and I decided to check out what movie was playing at the Tivoli theatre. It must have been one we didn't want to see, because we just walked back down the street and popped into the Club Cafe. We sat in one of the booths and ordered Cokes. We talked about my trip to Kelowna, wondering what it would be like with the boarding parents, the school, the teacher, and how many friends I would have by the end of the first week.

Passing the King George Hotel (now the Kokanee Inn) on the way back down the hill, we met Cisco and Mary Susan Alpine coming out. Cisco especially was bugging me about my girlfriend.

"What are you doing with her?"

Then Mary Susan started in. "Aren't the Indian women good enough for you, or is it the other way around?"

I tried to joke about it. "Oh, be quiet! Just because you don't have your guys with you."

"*Hiy*," they both said. "We're just letting loose."

By nine o'clock, we were back at the house. I think Brenda was feeling somewhat uneasy about my staying overnight and sleeping in the living room. It took me a long time to fall asleep but, when I did, I slept like a log. Brenda woke me up at five-thirty.

After coffee and toast, we headed out into the raw, brisk morning air. We hiked up the hill at a fast pace, up the main street of Creston to the bus depot. The regulars—loggers, truck drivers, and mill workers—were already sitting at their favourite tables having breakfast and drinking coffee.

The bus driver announced, "Anyone heading west, please board the bus. Leave your luggage beside the bus. Make sure it's tagged for your destination, and have your tickets ready!"

I looked at Brenda "Well, this is it. Let's go outside."

Waiting beside the bus, Brenda began to cry and so did I. We hugged each other for a long time. I don't know how long we remained locked together before we let go. I said to her again, "I guess this is it."

"Yeah, I guess this is it."

We hugged once more and kissed, and the empty feeling must have set in because she said, "I should go while I can still move."

"Me, too. I should find a nice seat to sit in so I can maybe get some more sleep."

She turned, waved, and walked away. I boarded the bus. I found a spot halfway down the aisle on the left-hand side. The bus driver collected my ticket and several others, took off his overcoat, placed it neatly behind his seat, and sat down. He released the air from the brakes, put the bus into drive, and we moved onto Canyon Street heading west.

It was still dark; the streetlights were on. The bus was the only vehicle driving down Creston's main drag on December 31, 1966. We were almost to the end of the street when I saw Brenda walking very slowly. As we passed, I waved and she waved back. Deep inside, I wanted the bus driver to stop the bus. I wanted to get off, but I couldn't say anything.

I felt pretty sad that I was leaving, but I felt good at the same time, knowing that things had to change for me because I'd seen enough, enough to know that life in the community was meaningless. Absolutely nothing was happening for the male members who could work. It seemed that the whole village was going through some kind of test, because people were dying left and right, not from natural causes, but because of alcoholism. The death rate was averaging three people a year, and our numbers on the reserve were dwindling.

7

SCHOOL IN KELOWNA

"ARE YOU CHRIS?"

Two girls were waiting for me on Ethel Street. I had phoned the Lunts to get directions, and it took twenty minutes to walk from the bus depot.

"Yes, that's me," I said.

They took me inside through the basement and upstairs into the kitchen, where I met Mrs. Lunt and her husband and Aunt Flo. They were all probably in their late fifties. Besides the two girls, there were also two boys living there. It was like an orphanage or a group home.

As we ate dinner, they told me the house rules. There were chores and I volunteered to do either the dishes or the vacuuming. Family laundry day was Wednesday, and we could have our washing done with everyone else's as long as our initials were on our clothing. Other than that, we were on our own, but we had to make sure Auntie Flo knew who was doing laundry on what day. Everyone had to be in bed by ten-thirty every night, and Mrs. Lunt said she wanted us home on Thursday nights for family dinner, Chinese food. I thought,

This is me at the age of nineteen attending VTS—Vocational Technical School—in Kelowna.

great! I loved Chinese food.

They also asked me a lot of questions. "What reservation are you from?...How big is it?...What tribe?...What language?...Are your parents still alive?...Do you have a girlfriend?"

I learned that Mr. Lunt worked for a dairy and left the house before six o'clock each morning. Mrs. Lunt worked as a waitress at the Dragon Inn Restaurant every day except for Sunday, Wednesday, and Thursday. Auntie Flo looked out for the rest of us. I thought the evening would never end, and I was exhausted by the time I unpacked my suitcase. I put my picture of Brenda on the night table beside the bed. I said my prayers and fell asleep immediately.

On New Year's morning, I sat on the bed looking around

This is Jerry, a real good friend, and cousin to my wife, Cecilia. He was the one who introduced me to Cecilia in the summer of 1967.

the room. It seemed to be an addition because it hung over the front porch, and it only had wallboard electric heaters. What really fascinated me were the electric blankets we had to keep us warm. I knew the other single bed in the room was for Jerry Gregoire, who hadn't arrived yet.

At breakfast I said Happy New Year and shook everyone's hands. There would be six of us going to school, three to senior secondary, one to intermediate, and Jerry and I to VTS. As I saw it, there were enough of us to keep the place hopping from morning until dusk. From that first day, I felt right at home, as though I had lived there before. After New Year's dinner, we pitched in to clean up and then watched "Star Trek," one of Mrs. Lunt's favourite programs. Jerry finally arrived around eight-thirty that evening.

I showed him to our room. Jerry thought it was neat having a front view of the street.

"Yeah," I said, "I like that you can watch people walk by."

"Where are you sleeping?" Jerry asked.

I pointed to the bed on the left side of the room and flopped down to watch him unpack.

"How come you took that side?" he asked.

"I've always done things from the left-hand side. Most Indians do things from the left side in a circular motion."

"Where did you learn that stuff?"

"From my dad and my uncle. Actually, you're born with it, and you gradually become more and more aware of it."

"Do you shave?" he asked.

"No, I haven't started yet."

"Well, you can use my shaving outfit if you decide you want to start growing hair on your face...Who's that?" He pointed to the picture on the end table.

"That's my girlfriend at home. Do you have a girlfriend?"

"No. My mom and sisters have this one particular girl they want me to go out with and maybe get married to someday. How many bedrooms in this house?"

"I think there's eight."

"What a castle!" said Jerry.

There was, however, only one bathroom in the house. I learned fast that it was on a first-come, first-served basis.

I certainly didn't mind the schedule that was beginning to unfold. Auntie Flo prepared breakfast each morning—usually porridge, toast, and coffee or juice. She also put out cold cereal if we wanted it. She made our lunches and left them on the counter with our names on them.

The first thing Jerry and I had to do was report to the registration office in the administration building for our schedules, list of supplies, and assigned classroom. We also received a map of the school showing the academic, business, and trade areas. If they wanted, students could buy food from a lunch wagon that would enter through a folding garage door on the east end of the recreation area. This was something unfamiliar to me. There were meat pies, hamburgers, fries, hot dogs, soups, candy bars, milk, juice, and pop—whatever people were hungry for. My mom had hooked me on meat pies when I was ten years old, so I told Jerry I would bring money the next day to buy a couple of pies.

I was registered in the Basic Training Skills Development program (BTSD), level II, which would give me an academic grade 10. From there, I could go on to level III, up to grade 12 equivalency, or into a skilled trade. About a month into the term, I had a personal interview and filled out an application stating what I wanted to do upon completion of the program. I decided my first choice would be to complete level III, my second choice was heavy duty mechanics, and my third was auto body repair.

The school work was easy at the beginning and gradually got harder. January and February went by very quickly. The instructor, Mr. Hoshisaki, told me that at the pace I was working I would easily finish level II by the middle of April. Jerry had a bit of trouble with the work, but with me on his back, he tried hard to keep up. I used to tell him if he didn't get going, I would be out of there and visiting him from the shop section.

After buying my school supplies and more clothes, I had very little money left in my savings account. I knew if I wanted my money to stretch, I'd have to hitchhike home once spring break came along. As it turned out, I did thumb my way home. I reached Osoyoos about eleven p.m. It had taken me six hours to go that seventy miles. The night was cold. While standing east of town at the foot of Anarchist Mountain, I heard several coyotes howling on the higher slopes. I had made up my mind to walk the hill, but after hearing those coyotes, I decided to head back towards the centre of town. Luckily, the driver of a freight truck surprised me by stopping.

"I'm heading to Creston," I said. "How far are you going?"

"Nelson," he answered. "Jump in and keep me company."

I don't recall the driver's name, but he was an angel that night. He handed me his thermos, and I poured myself a cup of hot coffee. The drive up the winding hill seemed to take forever, and that cup of coffee lasted the whole time. I fell asleep and didn't wake up until the driver applied the Jake brake as we were heading down into Grand Forks. When we reached Castlegar at about five-thirty in the morning, he said, "I'll let you off here because your chances of getting a ride to Trail are a lot better than if you go all the way to Nelson and on to Creston from there. There's more traffic on this stretch." (At that time, the highway over the mountain between Castlegar and Salmo did not exist.)

Within thirty minutes, a smelter worker on his way to Trail picked me up and dropped me off above the town. I walked briskly down the long flight of stairs to the city centre

and over the bridge that crossed the Columbia River, telling myself that my luck with rides would hold. Within a mile, a guy in a white van picked me up. He was on his way to Cranbrook on business. We talked about many different things in life, about taking risks. I told him I had wanted to walk the mountain at Osoyoos.

He said, "Chris, don't gamble! Don't gamble with your life like that. You never know what could happen to you."

Eighteen hours after leaving Kelowna, I reached Creston. I was so happy to be home, I ran into the little lobby of the King George Hotel and used the pay phone to call Brenda. There was a scream at the other end of the line when she realized I was not in Kelowna. When we met on the hill, we hugged. "Are you ever a sight for sore eyes and a lonely heart," she said.

At her house Brenda asked her mother to give me a ride home. "No problem," said her mom, who gave me a big wink. She and I got along really well; we were able to talk about a lot of things. We drove to Lower Kootenay in their 1952 Chev pickup. I was thinking about how different it would be at home without Dad. How was Mary doing with her baby Josie and my brother Rudy?

In the middle of the morning, the community looked as if it was still sleeping; there wasn't a soul walking around. Just another typical morning, I thought, no ambition here, everyone free to sit around the stove and make small talk.

I spent the two days at home visiting. Robert and I played pool and hung around the pool hall. Brenda and I talked a lot about school, about Kelowna, the friends I had met, the people I lived with. We reminisced about the summer, how we enjoyed each other's company and always found interesting things to do when we were together. We drank Coke and shared a plate of fries at the Kootenay Hotel café. I told her to plan on visiting me at Easter, that Mrs. Lunt had said she could stay there. All the time I was worrying about how I would get back to Kelowna. I knew from experience that it wasn't fun hitchhiking by myself. Perhaps I could borrow money for a bus ticket.

I phoned Bob Comfort from Brenda's house and told him my problem. He said, "Come on by tomorrow, and I'll have some cash for you." As we sat at his table drinking coffee the next day, he told me he was glad to help me out. "I know your dad would be proud of you if he knew you're making an effort to stay in school, Chris. He would come up with money for you if he was still alive."

"Yeah, I promised my dad that I would finish this time."

Bob handed me a twenty-dollar bill. "That's enough for your fare, plus something to eat on the way."

"Thanks," I said, "I will repay it."

"Maybe you can come home and throw a few bales of hay for me this summer!"

Saying goodbye to Brenda and people in the community wasn't as hard as it had been the first time. Something deep inside gnawed away at me, telling me to leave home, become somebody, be honest, gain respect, make a good life. As the bus headed out across the valley, I thought about my mom and dad, how each of them had had their own agendas for me. Dad wanted me to become a mechanic; Mom wanted me to be a priest. No sir! Before I had to make a choice in Kelowna, I didn't want to be monkeying around with a wrench, and I certainly didn't want to be drinking wine from a chalice. I brainstormed all the way to Kelowna, and when I stepped off the bus, I found myself glad to be back with my adopted family.

There were several new faces at school after the break. Jerry's sister Pauline was in the bookkeeping course and his cousin Lydia was studying in level III of BTSD. We all hung around together participating in school activities—Ping-Pong, volleyball, and pool—laughing and telling stories, and borrowing cigarettes from each other.

Jerry kept asking me to go home with him to Vernon. Early that year I did finally go to meet his family, who were members of the Okanagan Band. Getting to see their reservation life was quite an experience. It was similar in some ways to my life at Lower Kootenay, but the people I met with Jerry respected one another and were not hard-core alcoholics. They had vehicles and cattle and other things that my people talked about but didn't have because of our poverty level. The Okanagan people practised their traditions. They held winter dances, and I felt honoured to be able to participate. I was full of questions regarding their customs.

That first weekend at Jerry's, I learned what being a survivor was all about. I discovered that what was happening on my reserve was not the real world, but a place to ready yourself for death. My people were dying a slow death due to alcoholism.

After that I appreciated going to Vernon with Jerry every

second weekend. We were pretty good at hitchhiking, and it was getting easier as the weather warmed up. One Saturday in March we hitchhiked to Salmon Arm to watch the Annual Glen Eden Native Hockey Tournament. It was there that my hockey spirit was rekindled. I told Jerry that someday I would bring a team to the tournament. At that time there were six teams competing; today, the first fourteen teams that register get to play.

I always had fun with Jerry's family. They were always joking around. One time after lunch, Siggy's wife, Madeline, did the dishes. Since there was still no indoor plumbing, so no drain pipes (only a standpipe just inside the kitchen), Madeline asked me to empty the dishwater outside. I picked up the dishpan and headed for the door, which she opened for me. Just as I was stepping out, I felt a pinch on my butt. It straightened me right up! I glanced behind me and could only see Madeline. Imagine what went through my mind! I was afraid to take the dishpan back inside. It was many years later that Siggy admitted he had done the pinching.

I thought a lot about Jerry's family and how close-knit they were. I thought about how my family used to be like that but, since Dad's death, we had grown apart. I guess we were all feeling the loss and grief. Every two weeks I wrote to my own family—soon, that became once a month. All the time I was away, I probably received three letters from the family at Yaqan Nukiy. I wrote one letter each week to Brenda. She wrote back at least once a week, but the spark that we once felt for each other seemed to be dying. Easter came and went and no girlfriend. Nothing seemed to be going right for her; she told me that no one was co-operating with her and that

was why she didn't visit me. I took many long walks by myself that weekend, thinking of home, thinking of my friends, and thinking of Brenda. I found that walking could often overcome loneliness and depression.

Jerry had met a young woman from Penticton who was taking a secretarial course at the school. Their friendship led to walks, then to having lunch and dinner together, then to Jerry not returning home some nights. While he was making weekend trips with his new girlfriend back and forth from Penticton, I would be alone in Kelowna.

Sometimes they would invite me to go for walks with them. We'd end up at the park next to Okanagan Lake swinging on the swings. Just before dark we'd head back to the house for supper, wolf down our food, and Jerry would be gone again to visit his girl. I wasn't able to phone Brenda often, because Mrs. Lunt insisted I cut out long distance calls unless they were collect. With a budget like mine, my phone calls were next to none. Whenever I felt lonely, I'd listen to music. My favourite group was The Rolling Stones, and it still is today. The war in Vietnam was escalating, and I remember some of the news highlights were accompanied by Rolling Stones music.

In the meantime, I worked hard at school and made progress. I actually began to enjoy it, and I met Florence, who was a student from Kamloops. She was very nice-looking, had a super attitude, and handled herself well. We got along great. We went for walks and to movies together. The Lunts helped me celebrate my nineteenth birthday and said I could invite Florence. The family teased me about her and kept saying how good we looked together. From that day on, things got a lot more serious between me and Florence. Now it was my turn to say to Jerry, "Got a date. See ya later!"

I phoned Brenda to tell her we ought to call off our long-distance relationship, because personally I felt I could no longer maintain it. Brenda said she would remain hopeful and single, and we could maybe give it another try when I returned home. I said okay. In one sense I felt free, but in another I felt an obligation. I considered her response to be very thoughtful; not too many girls were like that. She definitely had her mother's caring and considerate nature.

May was just around the corner, and I dreaded the thought that Florence would soon complete her course and go home. I knew that I would never see her again once she was finished, and I was right.

I guess Jerry was one of the reasons I didn't finish my course when I could have. I knew I could write my final exam in late April, but I eased off and lost my focus. Although I was basically finished, I told my instructor I would write the exam during the second week of June.

"Why June?" he asked. "Why not the end of this month?"

"Well, I kind of want to wait for Jerry to get through some of the harder work, and I can give him a hand."

"You're sacrificing getting through and out by the end of this month for Jerry?"

"Yes, I am."

I got my way and didn't write the final exam until June.

8

THE GREAT WEEKEND

JERRY'S GIRLFRIEND HAD INVITED HIM TO LIVE WITH her in Penticton, but one weekend when he returned from visiting her, he said, "It's all over, Luke. We're finished." In a way I felt sad for him, but part of me was thinking, great, it's hitchhiking time again! The long weekend in May, Victoria Day, was probably the best weekend I've ever had.

Jerry and I started hitchhiking to Vernon on Friday after school. A couple of miles north of the Capri Centre, a vehicle passed us, slowed down, and stopped. We could see nothing but doors; it was a limousine and actually had four doors on each side. We looked at each other and started laughing.

"Which one?" I asked him.

We broke into another fit of laughter. We chose the last door and climbed in, still laughing, as our guts were sure feeling the humour of it all.

I whispered to Jerry, "To Vernon, James." And we laughed even harder.

The driver asked us where we were going and what we were laughing about. We explained it was just the size of the vehicle; it was hard to decide which door to open. After that, we used that story with our friends if we wanted something to laugh about.

On the Saturday morning, Jerry asked his family, "Anyone going to the Falkland Stampede?" No one answered. "Well, can I borrow a car? I want to take Luke to the stampede."

We got all duded up for the occasion; I even borrowed cowboy boots from Jerry's brother. His dad and mom each gave us $10 and told us to spend it wisely. Jerry didn't get a car, but we rode the thirteen miles north with his oldest brother, Leonard, and his family.

After eating breakfast in one of the only two restaurants in Falkland, we met up with one of Jerry's friends on the Falkland Creek bridge. His name was Charlie, and he was already getting liquored up. Jerry and Charlie began wrestling. Charlie, who was big and very strong, almost threw Jerry off the bridge. What I thought was fun seemed to be getting serious; I believed that Charlie really wanted to throw Jerry into the creek.

I hollered at Charlie, "Enough!"

"Who says?" He looked at me threateningly.

"I'm asking you to quit."

"You want me to throw you in the creek?"

"No, but you will probably try anyway."

As he walked towards me, I immediately got into my boxing stance.

"Tough guy, huh?" said Charlie.

"No, just protecting myself."

Jerry intervened at that point. "We're going to the stampede. See you later—you can finish what you started."

We never did see Charlie after that, which was quite all right with me. After the stampede, we went to a dance at the Falkland Hall, but didn't stay too long, as the band played nothing but country and western music. We did meet up with Willard Tonasket, another friend of Jerry's, who had come up from Oroville, Washington, where he worked in the orchards every year. Willard gave us a ride home at two in the morning.

The next day, he took us for a ride to his parents' place up on Grandview Flats, also known as O'Keefe Siding, and Jerry introduced me to more of his relatives. I was impressed with how big his family was. The Gregoire home and the Tonasket home were about four hundred yards apart, but the Tonaskets lived to the west of the Kamloops Highway and the Gregoires were on the hill overlooking the highway from the east side. Willard drove by two girls reading comics, lying on a blanket overlooking the highway. One of them was Jerry's cousin, Cecilia.

"What are you doing? What's her name?" asked Jerry, pointing to Cecilia's friend.

"None of your business," joked Cecilia. But then she said, "Petra, this is my cousin Jerry, and Willard, and I don't know who he is."

"This is my friend, Chris Luke. We room and board together in Kelowna."

Questions began to generate conversation between us and the girls. They wanted to know how old I was, but they didn't believe me, so I had to show them my ID.

"I thought you were about fifteen," said Cecilia.

"Well, I'm a genius. That's why I'm in college."

We spent the whole afternoon talking with the girls and decided to meet again that night to go to the drive-in movie together.

On the way back to Jerry's, he asked, "So, what do you think of Cecilia?"

"She's all right."

"Come on, Luke, you can do better than that."

"All right, she's good-looking and funny."

"Would you go out with her?"

"I'll think about it...What about Petra?"

Jerry didn't hesitate. "I'm in love."

"Boy, that was quick!"

During dinner that night, I witnessed the authoritarian side of Tommy Gregoire, Jerry's father. Jerry asked for the salt, saying, "Hey, pass me the salt."

Tommy glared at him and said, "My name's not Hey. I have a name, or you can call me Dad." Then he passed the salt and said, "Don't go running off tomorrow. I want you and Luke to do some fencing."

"Okay, Pops, we'll do it."

Willard picked us up at six-thirty. When we got to Grandview Flats, the girls were receiving last minute instructions from Cecilia's mother. We spent an hour or so cruising around town until the drive-in double feature started.

Just before nine, we found a good parking spot behind the concession stand and settled down to watch the movie. Willard was behind the wheel, Cecilia was up front beside him, I was directly behind Willard, with Jerry and Petra to my right. About halfway through the movie, Willard said he was tired and wanted to sleep, so Jerry told me to move to the front so Willard could sleep in the back. Then Jerry decided he and Petra should move to the front so Willard could have the whole back seat to himself. So, it ended up with the four of us across the front seat, Cecilia in my arms and Petra with Jerry. In a roundabout way, that night Cecilia and I had our first date, the beginning of a life together.

Early on Monday, the last day of our long weekend, Tommy was urging us on. "Hurry up, boys. The fencing can't wait."

He had already delivered the fence posts to Round Lake, where we were to do the repairs on a dozen or more posts. It took us all morning and most of the afternoon, but we got through in time to clean up and get to Falkland for the rodeo finals. Rodeos had always intrigued me, especially the bull riding—the fact that those riders could stay for an eight-second ride on such massive animals.

It was nearly dark when the rodeo finished, and Willard asked us if we wanted some beer. Jerry and I looked at each other. "Sure." Willard had fake ID from the States stating he was twenty-one years old. He did look twenty-one. He went into the Falkland Hotel and walked out with a case of Old Style beer. The three of us jumped into Willard's 1952 Pontiac sedan, cracked open a beer each, and headed for Vernon. When we reached Schweb's bridge, we turned left onto the Old Kamloops Highway, which runs four or five miles through reservation land. By the time we reached Willard's house, we'd had four beers each.

"If we're lucky, John might have some beer left," he said.

Willard's parents weren't home and his brother did have some more booze. I was beginning to love beer. I enjoyed it so much that I often went beyond just social drinking.

There was a knock at the door. Petra, Cecilia, and her sister Lydia had been waiting and watching, hoping we would come along. It was late, but Cecilia and I went for a walk anyway. I liked her and I knew she was fond of me. She was concerned about whether I would want to see her again. Was this just a weekend thing? She wanted to know. And what did I like about her? I told her I liked her attitude and her happy nature. I didn't tell her I was also mesmerized by her long, beautiful, black hair.

Jerry and I left early Tuesday morning for Kelowna. We had phoned Mrs. Lunt before we left Vernon, so when we got home we could just grab our lunches and head off to school. What a long day that was! I had every intention of hitting the sack early because I certainly was tired after that great weekend. But the phone rang.

"Chris, it's for you!" Mrs. Lunt hollered up the stairs.

I was a bit surprised to hear Cecilia's voice. She was calling from downtown Kelowna.

"What are you doing here?"

"Lydia had to come back to school, so I decided to ride along with her and visit you."

We had two hours to ourselves before Cecilia had to go back. We talked about my parents, the Yaqan Nukiy village, and the reservation.

"Do you have any other girlfriends?" she asked.

"Sure, I have girlfriends, but they're just friends."

"Lydia told me you have a girlfriend named Florence."

"Well, that was short-lived; we only saw each other while she was here."

"Don't you have any more feelings for her?"

"How can I? I knew when she left it was the last time I would ever see her."

Cecilia seemed satisfied with that, because she didn't want to begin a relationship with me if I had girls on the mind or in the field. After that first great weekend, we saw a lot of each other. I got to know her family better—her father Dave, her mother Edna, and her sisters and brothers, Lydia, Mary, Gerard, Anne, Raymond, David Jr., Simon, Bernadette, and Fabian.

Cecilia and I talked for hours when we were getting to know each other. I told her all about the interesting people I had met in my life, like my best friends, Robert Louie and Joe Pierre. We'd spent a lot of time hunting and fishing together.

"Robert used to play hockey, and I would double him on my bike for practices and games." I told her about all the times we had trouble with my single-speed bike. One night riding home we skidded halfway across the road trying to make a corner. My bike was wrapped around a telephone pole; we skinned our knees and elbows, and Robert ripped his new jacket. The front end of my bike had a bit of a twist that we couldn't straighten out.

When we got older, we used to play a lot of pool and go out on the weekends. One Saturday night after the drive-in movie, I was again doubling Robert on my bike. I had to make a quick turn to avoid a person who was walking on the back road of Erickson. The spot we turned into was mostly sand, and my front tire sank in because of the weight of the two of us. Robert flew off the bike in a forward somersault motion, almost landing on his feet. I lurched forward and ended sitting upright behind the handlebars, tight to the frame, my testicles in a lot of pain. I moaned and groaned for a bit, telling Robert over and over in various versions of the same thing: "I smashed my baby-maker!" While I was describing to him what had happened to my privates, he was rolling around on the ground laughing up a storm. The person we had almost run over came back to check on us. He was a Blackfoot from Brocket, Alberta, who was in the valley picking apples. We told him our story and he had a good laugh.

I told Cecilia about seeing Joe for the first time in church. My mom told me his name was Joe Pierre and his mother was in Vancouver. He was living with his grandparents, Johnny and Theresa Pierre. We both began school at the same time, in the same grade and classroom. Joe and I went through the same humiliation and abuse because of the colour of our skin. We were pals. We competed in track and field at school. We liked pole-vaulting so much that we built one that was eight feet high, and we used to clear it.

I remembered one time we went hunting early in the morning, so we packed a sizable lunch. When we stopped to eat, the sky darkened and I suggested we head home. Joe said no, that he still wanted to hunt. So we started gathering old short logs, placing them one on top of the other until they were high and wide enough for both of us to fit inside. It rained heavily, but our "German bunker," as we called it, served its purpose well. Suddenly, something moved under our feet—it was a snake that seemed to have two heads, one on the front and one on the back, something like a rubber snake. We both scrambled out of the bunker and stood in the rain, laughing like idiots, calling each other "chicken-shit." It wasn't that we were afraid of snakes, but that day we gave up our shelter to one that was black and double-headed.

I told Cecilia about my friend, Linda Robinson, and how she was an inspiration to me. How it was tough going to school only knowing the Ktunaxa language, and how Linda taught me English words and protected me.

"There was a girl named Pearl Ware. She was probably the toughest girl I ever met."

"What do you mean?" Cecilia asked.

"We ran into each other picking raspberries for Paul Popovich. I was bugging her by throwing raspberries at her and grabbing her picking can and running with it up and down the rows. Pearl would chase me and then give up.

"Anyway, she caught me by surprise and we started wrestling around, and she kicked my feet from under me. Down I went with her on top of me. I tried to squirm free, but she just didn't let up. I hollered for Robert to give me a hand, and I even hollered for Joe Skookum Jr. to get Pearl off me. Robert and Joe were both laughing at me because no matter what I did, she stayed right where she was.

"Pearl finally said, 'Are you going to quit bugging me? Quit throwing berries and grabbing my picking can?' I had no way out but to give in to her. 'Yes, I won't bug you anymore!' After sitting on me for another few minutes, she finally got up. Joe said he figured she knew me. 'Any other girl would have whaled on you,' he said."

I told Cecilia about my family and how we had grown apart.

We spent a lot of time with Cecilia's Uncle Pete and Aunt Josephine. The connection with them eased my loneliness and reinstilled the traditional values I was missing in my life. They were outdoor types, travelled a lot, and invited us to go with them. We picked *squmu* (saskatoons), *ɬawiyaɬ* (huckleberries), soapberries, gathered cedar roots, cut Christmas trees to make money, and went fishing. When the salmon were running, Pete took us fishing up the Salmon River south of Salmon Arm. Although it was a hot day, it was cool by the river, being shaded with cottonwood, poplar, and red willow trees. We ended up with three salmon, all weighing about five pounds. Another time he took us into a watershed area above Six-Mile Creek and we caught enough cutthroat to feed two families.

He told us a story about a time he and Josephine were driving home from picking huckleberries in the mountains. The station wagon was loaded down with the tent and other camping gear, pots and pans, and of course, huckleberries. The back end of the car seemed to be almost touching the ground, so at times it would sway a bit, as if the car was driving itself. At a spot just before the Old Kamloops Highway met the new one, a cop car was parked.

Josephine said, "Act like they're not there, Pete."

But Pete could see the red light flashing in the rear mirror. "Guess I can't act so good, because they're pulling us over. I guess the officer wants my autograph."

He pulled over to the side and rolled down his window. The RCMP officer approached the car. He bent over to look in the window at Pete.

Right away, Pete said, "I told my wife you stopped us because you want my autograph. Is that right, Officer?"

"I stopped you because you're swaying and driving over the white line."

"It's the huckleberries dragging my back end that's causing the sway. And I have a licence to drive on both sides of the highway."

"Wise guy," responded the cop. "And by the way, your dim is burned out. I'm going to have to write you a fix-it ticket." He checked Pete's driver's licence and wrote the ticket. "Now, get home, Gregory!"

When we stopped laughing at the story, I asked Josephine if he had really said those things to the officer.

She said, "Yes, and the only reason he got away with it was because the cop knew him."

Another time he was about to be thrown in jail for causing a disturbance at the local pool hall. Pete was skilled at pool, and he played for money. When the person he was playing refused to pay Pete what he owed him, he got angry and verbally abusive. The owner of the pool hall called the police, and they took Pete in for questioning.

On the way to the police station, Pete asked, "Are you going to can me?"

One of the officers answered, "With complaints of this sort, we keep a person for at least a couple of hours for safety reasons, to allow the person to cool off."

"Boy," said Pete, "it's going to be a very hard winter."

"Why is that, Gregory?"

"I've been told it's going to be a hard winter when you start canning Indians!"

Both of the cops laughed. "Where do you come up with these jokes? I'll tell you what, Gregory, we'll drive you home...and you stay home!"

All that spring, I was hitching from Kelowna to Vernon and back again, spending time with Cecilia and her family or jamming with Jerry in his basement. There wasn't a lot of time for school work.

On June 12, I wrote the final exam and the aptitude test on which I scored 121. I received my completion papers on June 16, 1967. As it turned out, I had finished level II with good marks, but there was no space left in the level III program. Heavy duty mechanics was full as well, so I was left with auto body repair, and I decided to pursue it. It would start in late July and end in the middle of November. I continued to work on the introductory lessons to level III until Jerry finished on June 26. Mr. Hoshisaki recommended I apply for the auto body course as soon as possible.

9

THE GOLDEN EAGLE

MY RETURN BUS TICKET TO CRESTON WAS STILL GOOD, and I wanted to be home in the middle of July. Luckily, before I left Kelowna, I had the opportunity to earn a few dollars thinning apples—not the best kind of work, but if you work hard enough, it pays. I put in a good five days and earned $50 for my efforts.

I'd had plenty of practice thinning, pruning, and picking apples in the Creston Valley orchards. Fred Nemanishen, a super guy, had taught me all about the various orchard jobs and he'd had confidence in my work.

I told Cecilia I thought it best that we break off our little engagement, because I wasn't sure I would be accepted into the auto body course, and I would probably return to Creston for good. We argued because she didn't like the idea of my leaving; she even threatened to follow me home. The result was that we broke up. My mind was on getting home, and nothing else mattered at the time.

One day Jerry came back from visiting Petra and said, "Cecilia's lonely. She really wanted to see you."

"If I see her again, I may never get home. There's nothing here for me. Back home I have friends and people I can go see for work."

I left Kelowna on a very hot day in the middle of July, feeling happy about my decision. For the first few days at home, Robert and I spent time playing pool, catching up on gossip, and swimming in the Goat River at the bridge. I wasn't a bad swimmer; I was one of those people who could stay underwater for probably a little over two minutes. I used to baffle some of the kids. I would grab a rock weighing at least ten pounds and walk around underwater for a good length of time before resurfacing.

One day at the river, I saw Brenda sitting on her beach towel. She called me over. "When did you get home?"

"Friday about midnight," I said.

"What did you do yesterday?" After I told her, she asked, "Why didn't you call or drop by?"

"I didn't have time."

"Of course, you wouldn't have time because you didn't make the time! You don't want to be with me."

"Hold on. How would I know that you still wanted to see me?"

"By phoning me!"

"Let's go have a dip," I said.

The next thing I knew, I was walking her home. We didn't have a lot to talk about. I think we both knew what was happening. I told her I would like to remain friends, and that was that.

As the weather turned even warmer, the Ministry of Forests issued fire warnings, and Robert and I registered at the Provincial Government building for firefighting. Two days later, Mike Janzen picked us up to fight a little spot fire up Blazed Creek and dropped us and Roy Ignatius on the highway with shovels, an axe, and one pack pumper. The burn was at least a third of the way up the mountain; it took us forty-five minutes to reach it. We chopped away at a couple of old snags and stumps into the roots to get at the source of the fire, which was the result of a lightning strike the evening before. It took us all day to finish the job, what with having to retreat down the mountain several times to refill the tank from the creek.

When we picked up our cheques the next day, I noticed I had received foreman's wages, which were a little more than what Robert and Roy got. Mike told us not to leave the country, because there was a much bigger fire near Kuskanook at the south end of Kootenay Lake. We had to be flown in by helicopter, and we fought that fire for three days.

In August I was made foreman of an all-Native crew to fight the Summit fire, which burned over two mountain ranges. Most of the guys who fought on that crew have now passed on: Stanley White, Steve Pierre, Pete White, Eddie Eugene, Frank Francis, Isaac Basil, Eddie Morigeau, and Joe Skookum Jr. Those still alive are Gus White, Roy Ignatius, Lloyd Basil, and Robert Louie.

The fires were spreading and springing up one after another throughout the valley. It was becoming mandatory for able-bodied people to join the crews. In the midst of the crisis, I received a letter from VTS informing me that my application for the auto body course had been accepted and that I would start the last week in August. I approached Mike Janzen with my news and he said, "Your education is worth a lot more than fighting fires. You'd better think of leaving soon." So I left the weekend before school started again. I had made about $270 in a little more than two weeks of firefighting.

I decided to hitch back to Kelowna. Roy Ignatius joined me because he was sick of fighting fires. We started at nine in the morning, split up when we got to the Okanagan, and I got to the Lunts at midnight. The next morning I headed for Vernon to see Jerry. After walking half a mile north, a car stopped beside me. It was Roy and some friends on their way to Enderby, so I got to Jerry's in no time. I really wanted to see Cecilia, but she wasn't home when Jerry and I got there.

"Tell her I was here to visit with her," I said to her mom.

"I don't think Cecilia wants to see you again. You really upset her when you broke off with her."

"Oh, I think she'll see me if she knows I'm here." I was remembering the letter I got from her a couple of weeks before. She had written that she missed me and was going to work it out somehow to visit me.

That evening I was at the store on Grandview Flats when I met up with Anne and Gerard, Cecilia's younger brother and sister. They were excited to see me, and I asked if Cecilia was home yet. Anne took off up the hill to get her. It wasn't long before Cecilia came flying over the top of the hill, and I mean flying.

In my mind, Cecilia was transformed into a beautiful Golden Eagle that soared over the crest of the hill and swooped down to settle on the ground in front of me before

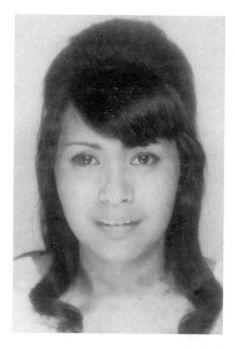

1967—Cecilia (Cil) Gregoire Luke at seventeen years of age— the Golden Eagle.

becoming whole again. I was the only one to experience this vision. Cecilia was unaware.

My dad told me that the Great Spirit works in many mysterious ways. "If you have it in you to dream, and your dream is good," he told me, "then wish upon that dream, and it will give you vision and guide you on your journey. It is the Ktunaxa way—when the Great Spirit decides to show you, he will show you." In my late teens I often wondered who my girlfriend, wife, partner in life was going to be, and here she was right in front of me. We hugged each other for a long time, as if we were old friends who hadn't seen each other for years.

During the first week of the auto body course, we learned classroom vocabulary and etiquette, became acquainted with the shop and the tools we would use. I discovered that welding was one of the major skills needed to succeed in the program.

I also discovered that there were several jerks in the automotive mechanics area but, like always, a little confrontation and people see their way clear. Ray and Shane, who were the same age as Jerry and me, lived just down the street from us. They were bigots. They had bad manners, swore a lot, and called people names. Nothing they ever said was good.

One morning on the way to school, Shane popped his head out of the window of his house and began screaming obscenities. "Hey, you fucking Indians! Where's the powwow happening today?"

"Go screw yourself!" I yelled back. "Get off your kick or I'll kick your ass!" I hadn't fought since grade nine, and this brought back memories of earlier years when fighting was a part of surviving in school: fights and more fights, always on the defensive.

Shane didn't quit shouting insults. I was feeling tough and thought I would teach him a thing or two. "Wait till after school and I'll kick your ass then."

All day long Jerry kept reminding me of the upcoming fight, but after school there was no Shane. A group of us walking home took our time passing his place; everyone was hoping he'd show. But it wasn't until a couple of days later that we caught up with him and Ray.

It took only three punches—a left jab, overhand right, and my power punch, a left hook—all to the chin. Shane was down for the count. I hadn't lost my boxing ability. We all milled around until he got up.

"Holy shit, what hit me?" he said. "Who hit me?"

"I did...Anyone else?" We all looked at Ray. "Nah, I don't think Ray wants to go. Do you, Ray?"

"No, I don't want to fight."

So that was that. We shook hands and tolerated each other for the balance of my time at school.

After that my school program rolled along smoothly. We had special assignments to complete and written tests based on the tools for specific jobs. I had a whole car to myself to work on, a 1955 Ford Classic four-door. The hood was dented beyond what I thought could be repaired. All the doors, except the one on the driver's side, had dents. After I removed the door panelling, I hammered out the dents; for five days I sanded and sanded that beast of a car. Along the way, I learned a few tricks of the trade. I restored the Ford to about ninety-five percent of its original shape. The owner, a collector, was proud of the way it looked when I finished with it.

Jerry owned one of the most awesome cars I've ever seen, and he used to bring it into the shop so we could take care of the few minor dents, scratches, and rust spots. It had belonged to his sister, Pauline, who gave it to him for his birthday. It was a 1955 Ford Victoria Crown two-door hardtop, turquoise blue and bone white, with convertible seating, a continental kit in back, chrome crown, automatic windows—just an excellent vehicle. The whole class wanted to work on Jerry's car whenever it was in the shop.

I didn't do well on my written exam—I got a C-, 59.5 per cent—but my shop mark was a B. The instructor told me I shouldn't have any problem gaining employment because I was a perfectionist on the practical side of things. Along with my completion certificate, he included a letter of reference. He wrote that I was reliable, conscientious, handled instructions well, and worked to perfection. He said that usually there were calls to the program from auto body businesses, but that he hadn't received any during this course. We were on our own.

Cecilia and I had been seeing each other every weekend and our relationship was changing. I started calling her Cil. We were talking about marriage. Her parents thought we were too young, but they agreed to it.

I had no one to vouch for me, so I wrote a letter to my sister Pauline, who was older than me. I explained to her that all I needed was her signature to show she was in agreement with the marriage. (In 1967 a person had to be twenty-one years old to sign for a marriage licence.) But I struck out with Pauline. She had always been the type of person who thrived on being right and who was very argumentative, especially when it came to proving her point. I used to think she would make a good sergeant in the army, a crime investigator, or a lawyer. When anyone crossed her path, she would surely let them know what she thought about them. She was stubborn and tough as nails, but that was the same with our whole family. She refused to sign any papers and told me I should wait. She reminded me that Dad would have wanted me to do it the Indian way—to know each other and live with each other for a whole year. If Cil and I still felt the same way about each other in a year's time, then she would sign the papers.

Around Christmas, I moved in with Cil's family. I prepared job applications with my resume and references and made several copies to deliver to various auto body shops in the Okanagan. They all said business was slow. The owner of a shop in Armstrong said hiring was out of the question. I checked with the employment centre in Vernon to see if any jobs were available, but there was nothing.

I began feeling depressed and homesick, thinking about Dad, wondering if the family would have a feast and give-away to honour the one year since his death. Would they give special thanks to the Great Spirit, the giver of life, as we always did on our birthdays? We gave our respect instead of gifts, in appreciation for another year of life.

I later discovered that none of the traditional ceremonies were practised that year, either to remember my father or to bring in the New Year. One could say that the culture of the Lower Kootenay died spiritually in 1967.

10

SIX MONTHS IN KELSO

I WAS WISHING I COULD JUST GET UP AND LEAVE. IT WAS important to me that Cil be with me, and she understood the Ktunaxa tradition about being together before marriage, but her mother made it absolutely impossible for her to leave with me unless I had a job and a place to live.

My youngest sister, Doreen, was keeping in touch by writing from St. Eugene's residential school in Cranbrook. She told me I was a brother she looked up to. She said it was good being away from home, especially with all the drinking that was going on with the band. In February of 1968 I heard she had dropped out and was living with Pete White, whom she married later that year. She confided that she was pregnant. They moved to Kelso, Washington, where Pete had a job with Weyerhaeuser, one of the largest logging companies in the U.S. I wrote to her, asking what the job situation was in Kelso, which was just north of the Oregon border on the Columbia River. She spoke to Pete and he arranged for me to start work the last week of April. Being Native Indians, we were able to live and work in the United States without acquiring a work visa.

To earn my keep at the Gregoires I had been chopping wood and doing various other chores. On occasion, I went hunting and managed to bag a three-point whitetail buck. I was checking in at the employment office and the Department of Indian Affairs in Vernon twice a week. Through Indian Affairs I learned of the new housing that was planned for the Lower Kootenay community to begin in the fall. My biggest concerns were what would happen to our old house and who would get the new housing. I learned through Doreen that Mary would be one of the recipients. I wondered then what would happen to the rest of us in the family if we ever decided to return home. I wrote several times to Mary, but she didn't answer my letters. I wrote to Pauline, who wrote back and said, "As you know, I don't live down at the Mission anymore, so I don't know what's going on. If I find out anything, I'll let you know." Then she went on about the weather and how Creston now had a radio station and about who had died recently.

Cil spoke to her parents about going with me to Kelso. She was matter-of-fact about it, saying, "If you don't let me go, I'll run away anyway." The discussion became heated, and I didn't appreciate the attention I was getting. I certainly didn't want to come between Cil and her family.

Cecilia was only eighteen years old at the time, so now I can understand her mother's concern. A few days later, she came to me and said, "I want you to look after her, treat her good. Make sure you stay in touch. If it's too rough to be on your own, you can always come home."

It helped that Doreen sent a money order for $250 in U.S. funds to pay our transportation. She told us to take the bus to

Spring 1968—
This is Cil and I
enjoying each
other at our
home in Kelso,
Washington,
where I worked
for six months.

Wenatchee and then the passenger train to Kelso. The final days at the Gregoire residence were hectic. Nobody wanted Cecilia to leave, and Cil herself started getting cold feet.

"Maybe you should go on ahead and I'll come later when you're settled in," she said.

"I don't like that idea. You'll be travelling alone. It won't be bad travelling with me now." Even I was feeling a bit uneasy about the unknown. All the "what-ifs" popped up and the "should-haves" were not far behind.

We were able to get a ride with Jerry and his brother Leonard as far as Oroville. They were both working in the orchards. At the time, Jerry didn't appear to be in good health. He was pale and strung out. He told me he was just under the weather, but he looked worse than that to me.

That night my suspicions were confirmed. We were

awakened in the Oroville pickers' shack by a loud thud at about two in the morning. Jerry had fallen off the couch. He said he was in pain. Leonard and I were worried he might be having an appendicitis attack so we drove him all the way back to Canada, thirty miles to the nearest hospital in Oliver, because the U.S. hospitals did not accept B.C. medical cards, especially those of Native Indians.

At the hospital Jerry was rushed to the emergency room. Not much later, a doctor told us that Jerry was going to be okay, but he wouldn't be picking any fruit for a day or two. On the return trip to Oroville, Leonard and I speculated on what could have been Jerry's problem, but it's still a mystery to me. That night I only managed to squeeze in a couple of hours sleep.

Cil and I boarded the bus for Wenatchee the next morning. I had never been that far south of the border, so this was all new and frightening in the sense of taking a risk and exploring at the same time. We were two very young people heading into obscurity, not knowing what to expect. The urgency to be alone together was the driving force for both of us. I assured Cecilia I loved her and we would be fine.

Unfortunately for us, the train had just left when we got to Wenatchee, but we were able to catch a bus to Seattle, where we had a two-hour layover. We arrived in Kelso, about 230 miles south of Seattle, at three-thirty in the morning, but Pete and Doreen got up and made coffee, happy that we had made the trip with few problems.

Our Kelso experience lasted only six months, but I'll never forget it. The company outfitted me with caulk boots, tin pants (actually double-layered canvas pants), gloves, and rain gear, then would gradually deduct the cost from my pay cheques in small amounts. I was already in debt before I put my first day of work in. I would be making $3.65 an hour, which I thought was excellent pay.

It took me a while to get the hang of high-lead logging. The trip to Klamath Camp took an hour and a half, then it was another hour to the logging area. Because I was a green-horn, the first two weeks just about killed me. I was in bed by 8:30 each night after working a twelve-hour day: all that mountain air, the running around packing chokers tired me out. I first started working with a fellow named Stan behind the Caterpillar pulling a yoke that was flying three chokers. Lenard was the Cat operator. We were working in an area of freshly cut timber; we were supposed to clear the landing and prepare the timber deck, removing any timber that might obstruct the yarder and tower. Stan told me we were called chasers, because as soon as the rigging dropped to the ground, we would run and wrap chokers around the logs so the yarder could pull them to the landing. Stan was a practical joker; he'd do anything for a laugh. On my first day he played a trick on me, one of the oldest tricks played on green-horns like me. It was a slack time in the afternoon, and he told me to hurry down and get a choker stretcher from George before Lenard got back with the Cat. I ran like a fool to the landing, almost falling on my face a few times.

"Stan needs a choker stretcher!" I hollered.

George laughed. "Tell Stan to go screw himself!"

So I repeated that to Stan, and he said, "That son of a bitch. He wouldn't give you a choker stretcher, eh?"

"He doesn't have one," I said.

It wasn't until a week later that I told Pete about the incident, and he informed me there was no such thing. I felt like a real dummy.

One morning I was assigned to a rigging crew, the only one still using the spar tree with a yarder on tracks. (All the other yarders were on rubber tires with steel poles connected to each other to form the spar pole and they were self-driven.) The foreman of my crew, Clarence (nicknamed Click), kept to himself and didn't say much. He would watch us from the top of the landing, and then we wouldn't see him until we boarded the crummy to head down to the main camp. Click was known as the bull hooker. He'd put on spurs and climb the spar tree to wrap it with a pulley block for the mainline and wrap the mainline (butt rigging) to the haulback lead wire through blocks secured to stumps fifty or sixty feet apart at the end of the clearcut. The area inside the two blocks, inside the curve of the cables, was called the bight because of the possibility that either the mainline or the haulback might snap, or the blocks could give way. I understood the danger right away, because as soon as the slack was taken up by the yarder, I could see the tension and hear the wires—especially the haulback—make that whipping sound. I know that a couple of guys got caught in the bight. One lost his life and the other had both legs broken. Our rigging slinger, Allen Smith, who was in charge of the chokermen, always made sure we were outside the bight before he signalled the yarder operator to go ahead. This was high-lead logging.

I enjoyed working with this crew. I learned the signals in a hurry and was given the responsibility of packing around the bug, the pocket transmitter that was used to communicate with the yarder operator. As a result, I got a wage increase. Click was teaching me all about being a bull hooker. I even had the opportunity to put on spurs and a waist strap and climb a hundred-foot spruce tree. When I glanced down, my heart jumped into my throat.

One day a Japanese group arrived in a chartered bus to tour the main camp and surrounding area. Click was asked to demonstrate. It took him all of three minutes to get up the tree and start sawing off the top. When the top crashed to the ground, the Japanese visitors applauded Click. Next, he tied himself to the tree and sat on the trunk as it swayed back and forth. He climbed down after five minutes and everyone shook his hand. When they left in their bus, Click said to me, "I haven't done that in a long time. Sure gave me a rush."

The boss said, "That was really impressive, Click, but don't you ever do it again!"

Payday was every two weeks. After my first pay, I was able to buy some food to share with Pete and Doreen. By the end of April, Cil and I were living in our own apartment and could buy our own food and linen for the bed. We even started repaying Pete for his generous contribution to our travel money.

In the evenings, Cil and I would take long walks over the two bridges—the one over the Cowlitz River and the quarter-mile span over the Columbia—to enjoy the air and the scenery. We'd go window shopping in Longview, which was just next door to Kelso. A couple of times we went to a show;

one was called "Billy Jack," an excellent movie about the Indian movement and the freedom to exercise rights. Every Friday evening we ate supper at a nice little restaurant called the Corner Café a block from our apartment. The people who ran it were super. Before we got there, they didn't know about fries and gravy, but soon there were customers ordering "Chris-fries-and-gravy." They actually named it after me. I told them it was a Canadian thing, but it became a popular side order in Kelso, Washington.

I really wanted to take Cil to Creston for the Blossom Festival, which happened every year on the long weekend in May. I got time off and we bought return train tickets from Kelso to Bonners Ferry, Idaho. After catching the bus from Bonners to Yahk and waiting three hours for the bus to Creston, we had been travelling for twenty-four hours. We spent the night with Pauline, who was living in the Goat River Bottom with Speed Benny in a cabin that had no running water. But Speed had filled a hot water tank and connected it to the bathtub, so all you had to do was turn on the faucet and add a pail or two of cold water. Before we took baths, we had to be sure to refill the tank for the next person.

The next morning Cil and I hiked to Yaqan Nukiy so she could meet Mary and Rudy and a few people in the community. The village had changed a little because some of the houses had been torn down—those that were not being lived in. We didn't stay long. Robert joined us and we headed to town to watch the parade. The streets were crowded with people who later gathered at the north end of the high school field to listen to several of the marching bands performing. The fife and drum band from St. Eugene's Mission school in Cranbrook and the Kimberley Pipe Band were the most entertaining and colourful to watch.

The midway that came to town every year with its games and rides, sideshows, and food stands was set up in the middle of the school field. We had a burger and rode on a few of the more breathtaking rides. Then I made a big mistake. I got conned into playing one of the "skill-testing" games, a machine-operated football game. I was hooked, gaffed, and in the boat before I realized what happened. Eighty-six dollars later, all I got for my effort was a stuffed twenty-dollar bear that we called Sucker Bear.

"You've got this rigged," I said to the guy running the machine. "You definitely ripped me off."

"You got a stuffed bear worth twenty bucks and, if you put another five dollars down, you'll probably get to the end zone. Then you can trade the bear for one hundred U.S. dollars."

"No way. You already took all my money."

"You'd better leave," he threatened, "or I'll have someone call the police."

I felt defeated. In a matter of twenty minutes, I had used up all our weekend money on one stupid game. The guy's voice echoed in my mind along with the voice of the person who had given me a ride during spring break the year before. I remembered clearly what he had repeated several times. "Don't gamble, Chris."

We sat on the school steps. Cecilia was staring at me and

mimicking the guy who had ripped me off. "Well, what do you figure, *Sport*?" She still had a bit of the money that we had kept back to use to get to Bonners Ferry and overnight in a motel on the way back to Kelso.

"It's not all that bad," I said. "If we can get a ride to Bonners, we can probably stay at my dad's aunt's place. But we can't tell anybody what happened and why we're on foot. It's embarrassing."

When we got back to Pauline's, she and Speed were both drinking and my niece Josie was with them. Mary had dropped her off for the night so she could go out and celebrate her birthday. We were almost asleep when Pauline started raising her voice.

"If you don't stop complaining," she said, "I'll take Josie and walk to the Mission to drop her off and I won't come back tonight!"

"Don't be foolish," said Speed. "It's cold out. You can't take the wee girl out this late."

Straight as an arrow and smart as a whip, Pauline told Speed that Josie certainly wasn't "wee" and it probably wouldn't be the last time she would be out in the dark and cold late at night.

"Well, it's not going to be on my conscience if something happens to her," Speed answered.

"What conscience? You don't even have a conscience."

The argument wound down with Speed telling Pauline to be quiet because there were people sleeping in the next room, and Pauline telling him we were probably listening to everything that was being said. Eventually, everything was quiet and nobody went out in the dark.

I took a good look at the village as we passed by Sunday morning on our way south. It was very peaceful. Smoke was curling up from a few chimneys. Things would soon be changing, as new homes would be springing up in the fall.

I tried to get a ride to Bonners Ferry with Zachary Basil, but he didn't have any money for gas. So Cil and I started hoofing it. After five hours, when we had reached the Mission Creek store fifteen miles north of Bonners Ferry, the Shottanana family stopped for us and gave us a ride into town. We missed the train by an hour and a half. The next one would leave on Monday at noon.

As planned, we stayed with Dad's Aunt Helen and her husband Baptiste, both in their mid-sixties. We talked about the Yaqan Nukiy community and the new housing. Only a couple of homes and the church would be left; all the others would be demolished. Helen said it was sad that her Kootenai village had not been under federal government protection in the fifties and sixties. It had no Reserve status and was supposed to have been phased out long ago. She told us that the government, namely the Bureau of Indian Affairs, leased out most of the tribe's property without direct input from tribe members. (The Bonners Ferry Band finally received Reserve status in 1975.)

As Cil and I waited for the train at the depot, I thought about all the changes in our lives—how the passenger train used to pass through Creston and continue on up the Columbia Valley, how Doreen and I used to take the train back to school in Cranbrook. And how here I was leaving home again, not knowing when I would return.

I got back to work in Kelso a day later than expected. I was dreading having to wake up early again. Once back at camp, though, the scenery and clean air definitely changed my attitude. A month later I put in my bid to be a rigging slinger and got the position, which paid fifty cents more an hour. I was responsible for my own crew of four men who set chokers and I "packed the bug," which meant I signalled the yarder operator where and when to place the butt rigging. I learned quickly and, in one eight-hour shift, my crew accomplished the ultimate—we yarded in 278 logs. On a normal working day, the crews would yard about two hundred logs. We were rewarded with free dinners for ourselves and our families.

Cil's sister Lydia arrived to stay with us and find work in Kelso. She picked strawberries and eventually got jobs doing housecleaning. She earned good money and helped pay the rent and buy groceries. Doreen and Pete were making plans to move back home because Doreen was pregnant and due at the end of August. We often went out with them. Pete had bought a 1955 Pontiac and he invited us to take a ride with them down the coast to Portland before they left. The scenery along the ocean was fabulous. We visited the Grotto, an altar that protruded out of a rock wall, with statues of Christ and the Apostles, the Virgin Mary, and Joseph. We toured the church and flower garden and gift shop. We bought presents

Fall 1968—Cil and I getting ready to head home to Vernon from Kelso.

for Cil's mom and I got a Saint Christopher medal, which I still have today. It was special to be there, to see the beauty, to feel the spirit and comfort of the Creator. I experienced a connection that could never be matched.

When Pete and Doreen left, I felt a loneliness inside. At the end of September Cil and I planned a dinner for all of the friends we had made in Kelso, and I quit work the first week in October.

We travelled back to Canada by train, but this time went via Seattle and Vancouver. At the border, we had to go through Customs and declare our belongings. Our suitcases caused no trouble, but it was the box of utensils, dishes, pots, and pans that the official was having a problem with. Sometimes telling the truth can be stressful. I explained to him that as a Native North American, I could live and work in the United States, own a car, own property, and travel back and forth without having to obtain any type of visa. The dishes and other utensils, I said, were all a part of living and working in the U.S. I told him to check the U.S. Customs Act, especially the section dealing with Native Americans.

In frustration I said, "I can leave the pots here until you decide what you want to do." Cil and I got ready to walk away.

"Wait a minute," he said. "I'll check with my supervisor."

When he came back, he changed his tune. "You're right. This is your property, and you can work without getting a visa from the U.S. government. Sorry for the inconvenience. Thanks for being patient."

The rest of the trip, by Greyhound to Vernon, was less stressful, but tiring. Fifteen minutes after I phoned him, Jerry was at the bus depot to pick us up. It was a wonderful feeling to be back. Cil and I were going to be busy in the next month. We had to plan our wedding.

11

DO YOU LOVE THIS WOMAN?

IN OCTOBER OF 1968 CIL AND I STARTED MAKING arrangements for our marriage. We went to church one Sunday morning with her mother—a devout Catholic who would find a Mass to attend every week no matter where she was—because we needed to speak to the Reverend Father Devlin. As it turned out, we had several visits with him.

We also had to meet with the lawyer, who set up meetings with the magistrate, so we could receive consent to get married. A week before the wedding, there was one final appointment. There were three lawyers and the magistrate besides Cil and myself.

They asked Cecilia three questions about our relationship: Do you love this man? Are you ready to marry this man? Are you ready to live the rest of your life with this man? They asked me the same three questions about "this woman" and we both answered yes.

It was a beautiful sunny day on November 16, the day Cil and I got married. Relatives and friends crowded into St. Benedict's Church at Head-of-the-Lake on the Okanagan

Indian reservation. Jerry, my good friend and best man, was late. We had celebrated the night before; when I left, he and my other friends were still partying. When he did arrive, he looked bleary-eyed. He was working on his tie, and I noticed he wasn't wearing socks.

"Where are your socks?" I asked.

"In my pocket," he mumbled.

"Never mind them. Let's get started."

As we stood at the altar, I asked, "What happened to you?"

"Oh, Luke, it was a long night. We partied until four-thirty." He gave me that funny grin.

As the procession started, I looked to the back of the church. Cil's sister Mary was the bridesmaid, and her baby brother Fabian also walked down the aisle, holding onto his dad's pants.

Then, it was as if I was part of the congregation staring at this beautiful woman dressed in a light blue lace dress and veil who came toward me down the aisle on the arm of her father. Suddenly—snap—she was standing next to me. What a feeling! When I think of that particular moment, I believe I actually had an out-of-body experience—all that anxiety and hype that go with getting married.

The wedding procedure and vows did not last long. Before I knew it, we were signing the marriage certificate and regis-ter. Outside the church, everyone greeted us. The one negative thought that kept coming to mind was that no one from my family or my community was there to celebrate with me. However, I thought of it this way: when we visited during Blossom Festival in May, I had introduced Cil and we had received the approval of the elderly ladies of Yaqan Nukiy.

Most of the Gregoires and several friends joined us for a luncheon that Dave and Edna had arranged. We sat around talking and laughing with everyone for a couple of hours before we decided to change into more comfortable clothing. Since my wedding day, I have never worn a suit jacket or tie, and I have no plans to ever wear them again.

Cil and I do plan to remarry, to renew our vows tradition-ally. In a traditional marriage, grandparents and parents were involved in directing the future lives of the bride and groom. On a specific day, the young man would be invited to call on the bride-to-be and to stay several weeks with the family. Then the couple would go on to live the same amount of time with the groom's family. When it was thought the couple was compatible, feasts were exchanged and the young people would be showered with gifts. They were married by the com-munity spiritual leader and remained at one of the family homes until it was thought safe for them to live on their own.

Another tradition that was readily accepted was the cere-monial dance, in which young men and women chose each other for marriage. The same family involvement would take place. A Ktunaxa custom that is no longer followed stipulated that a widow marry the brother of her deceased husband; the widower would marry the sister of his deceased wife. Divorces in the community needed the consent of the elders.

The responsibility of marriage falls not only to the couple but also to the entire community. People who attend the wed-ding are automatically witnesses and take responsibility for the future of the married couple. "It takes an entire commu-nity to raise a child," and in the same way, it takes an entire community to support a couple.

As I write this, I look back at where Cil and I were as teenagers, what we have done, what we've accomplished together, how much we've grown mentally, emotionally, and spiritually. I look at the gifts that we have received spiritually and physically. We are gifted with five beautiful children and thirteen grandchildren. I love each child and grandchild with a unique personal love. I cherish each of them as my own.

Cil and I have been together since that day the Golden Eagle appeared to me in a vision. Our love for each other remains strong; we share the ups and downs, the tears, and the laughter.

12

INQUALLA

DURING THE SIX MONTHS IN 1968 THAT CIL AND I WERE in Kelso, I missed playing music with our little band, but we picked it up again in November. We played that year on New Year's Eve at Head-of-the-Lake.

The group had started when Jerry and I were going to VTS. Whenever we were in Vernon, we spent a lot of time in Jerry's basement. He would pick up his guitar, and I would jump in behind his drum set, and we'd start to jam.

We'd play our favourite tunes: "Louie, Louie," "Gloria," "I Can't Get No Satisfaction," and "House of the Rising Sun," to name a few. I guess we formed the band when people noticed I could play a mean set of drums. Willard handled bass and sometimes lead, while Jerry played mostly rhythm and lead. I was the lead singer, with Jerry and Willard harmonizing. We were the threesome, Inqualla, named after the Chief of the Okanagan Nation, who lived at Head-of-the-Lake. This was the origin of my musical career. We became one of the hotter bands in the Okanagan, especially because we came from the reservation.

Jamming at Jerry's became a ritual, especially when I was helping him with yard and corral work, mostly fencing. We would play together every chance we got. Jerry would start plucking on his guitar. I would light a cigarette for myself and ask Jerry if he wanted one. "Sure, light it for me, Luke." He would take a couple of puffs and place the cigarette between the strings and neck of the guitar and continue plucking. Maybe the tune was "Mrs. Brown, You've Got a Lovely Daughter," by Herman's Hermits.

I'd sit on the stool behind the drums and set my cigarette on an ashtray I had sitting on a chair next to the floor tom. I'd pick up the sticks from the snare drum and begin to put out a 4-2-4 beat, then switch to a simple 2-1-2, and then to a 4-4. Jerry would automatically start a tune that matched the beat. We kept it simple and didn't drown each other out.

Musicians used to comment how unorthodox I was, that I didn't play the drums as they're supposed to be played. I'm left-handed, but I didn't change the setup. Playing left-handed, I felt freer to do drum rolls.

Martin Wilson, who was twenty years our senior, was like our manager. He had riding stables and ran trail rides out of his home. Without him, we wouldn't have had the equipment and P.A. system, which he provided by putting his riding equipment up for collateral. I appreciated Martin for his knowledge and his caring ways; he was one of those people who continued to practise the traditions of his people.

Occasionally, we'd stop at his little log house for a cup of coffee. "Hey, Martin," said Jerry, on one of those visits, "wanna come over to the house, have supper, and listen to some good music?"

"What music?" asked Martin, laughing.

"Us, Martin, us!" said Jerry, pointing at me and then at himself.

We picked up Willard, who was complaining that he thought we were never going to show up.

"Quit your bitching," said Jerry. "Let's go."

"You'll have to run me home; my bass guitar is up at Mom and Dad's."

"What's it doing up there?" Jerry snapped.

"Whoa, Boss, look who's sounding bitchy," said Willard.

Martin said to me, "Boy, don't those two sound like they're married to each other."

This comment got Jerry going. He looked at Martin and said, "My heart, my heart…I think I'm dying!" He told us the story about the accident that happened earlier in the year when he was driving Martin home. The snowdrifts were something to see. Especially on the secondary roads, the snow sometimes covered half the route, making it single-lane traffic in many places. According to Jerry, he lost control of the wheel when the car hit one of those drifts, sailed over the bank, and landed in the ditch. Jerry was laughing about it now. "I hollered 'Whooie!' and Martin had his hands on his chest, saying 'My heart, my heart. I'm dying!'"

Martin started laughing, too, but he said, "Damn you, *slaux*, you weren't supposed to tell anyone about that."

We piled into Jerry's car and retrieved Willard's guitar. Supper was ready when we got back to Jerry's. His mom, Mary, said to all of us, "Better eat before you make noise." This was her opportunity to get some words in while she still had Jerry's and, I suppose, our attention. As she was talking,

Jerry began to hum a tune. She spoke louder and Jerry hummed louder, until finally he grabbed his mom by the arm and started dancing with her. She broke out in a stomach laugh while they waltzed around the room. I hadn't ever witnessed anything like this in my life. It was funny but sweet. They had a mother-son relationship that was unique. It brought back memories of different times I had played tricks on my mother—hiding the axe on her, switching the pails of grain for the horses, even growling like a grizzly behind some bushes while picking huckleberries above Kid Creek. She would just say, "Quit making noise. Pick berries."

About six-thirty, Perry Joe, a cousin of Jerry's, showed up. (He had joined the band after we had put on our second dance.) We sat around smoking and talking in the basement. Jerry and Willard plugged in their amps and guitars, running their fingers through the strings, tuning them. Perry set up the piggyback on the P.A. system and was testing for sound. He positioned the mike stand for himself and put the other mike next to me, setting up the boom bar so I didn't have to move while singing. Perry was my backup and harmonizer; he had shakers and a tambourine.

We started strumming and got the beat going. When we were all warmed up, we ran through the songs we knew and then worked on new material. Three hours later, Martin checked his watch and yawned. "Good practice," we all agreed.

At the beginning, we only knew about twelve songs, and it takes at least seven for one hour of teen dancing. We would perform seven songs, take a break, and then play the balance of our repertoire. In the last hour, we would repeat the songs the crowd liked best.

A few hours before each dance, I would get butterflies. When I was boxing, I used to have anxiety attacks. The excitement would be overwhelming. Once, when I was boxing in Spokane in the Inland Empire championship, I was so hyped that, during weigh-in, the doctor told me to sit in a tub of cool water for half an hour to lower my blood pressure. I did, and my blood pressure returned to normal. (The ref stopped the fight in the third round anyway, because I had a nose-bleed that wouldn't stop.)

While I was playing and singing with Inqualla, the excitement before each dance would build, and I would become impatient to get going. Different lyrics would scramble in my head, and I would get agitated. I learned to take a relaxing bath before each performance.

At the end of 1968 we were gaining popularity. At the New Year's dance, people told us we were doing a great job, that we had improved a lot since they'd last heard us. Since I was doing most of the vocals, we had Newman Gottfriedson, Jerry's nephew, do the drumming. Newman could carry a good beat. We opened as usual with "Poor Side of Town" as performed by Johnny Rivers and followed it with "I'm Not Your Stepping Stone" by the Monkees. My favourites at the time were "Hey, You've Got to Hide Your Love Away" by the Beatles, "Don't Let Me Be Misunderstood" and "We've Got to Get Out of This Place" by the Animals, and "Knocking on Heaven's Door" by Bob Dylan.

During the breaks, there was hardly time for a few gulps of beer before we heard, "Hey, guys! Let's get going, guys!" and Jerry would be strapping on his guitar again. We got a lot of requests and repeats, and played until the grand finale, "Gloria," at two-thirty in the morning. We made $240; split five ways, we each ended up with $48. It was in the extra hour at the end of most dances that we earned our money. We would charge $100 to play for the evening, but the hat would be passed for extra time and we'd end up with twice as much.

We played at a few benefit dances, one for the Head-of-the-Lake Stampeders Hockey Club, who were fund-raising to off-set tournament fees. We started getting offers to do gigs in Vancouver, Chilliwack, and Mission but never accepted, as we didn't think we were good enough.

More and more, I was thinking about going back to the Kootenays to live. "I feel bad about leaving," I said to Jerry. "We have such a good thing going with the band. You'll have to carry on."

"I don't know about that," he said. "You know that Perry won't go on without you. I don't know what Willard and Newman are going to do."

Cil is a wonderful person with a big heart. She can sense things more readily than I can. "After we leave, Chris," she said, "the band will no longer be together. Jerry will try to keep going, and maybe there will be different people…What are you going to do when we move to Creston and you get the urge to sing and play drums?"

"I don't know. Hopefully, I can do something about it."

As it turned out, Jerry had a totally new band by 1971.

13

GOING HOME

THE NEW YEAR CELEBRATIONS MADE ME THINK ABOUT tradition and my own home in Creston. My thoughts ran wild as I wondered about the people at Lower Kootenay. How many had brought the New Year in with a bang? Was there anyone still celebrating traditionally?

As a child, I had looked forward to the New Year. Just before midnight, the women would take their buckets of food to the home of the spiritual leader (called the church chief) for a celebratory meal. The next day would begin with the men coming together in front of the church for a prayer before they shot off their guns three times. Everyone in the village then attended Mass if there was a priest, or a service led by the church chief. A communal meal followed with a presentation about the need to maintain our way of life and to be vigilant during the next twelve months. Afterwards, the men and women lined up separately and followed along as each household was blessed, with hopes for prosperity and good health.

The New Year's celebration is now very different, but there

are those who grew up with the custom who still follow it.

I was thinking all the time now of going home. Absolutely nothing was happening for me in the job market in Vernon, except for a few odd jobs for neighbours: feeding the cattle, chopping wood, cleaning out barns, or shovelling grain. We were helping out Cecilia's family with groceries when we could, but our savings were dwindling. I told Cil there was no way we were going to ask for some subsidy.

I continued to search for a job, making frequent trips to the employment centre. When I filled out my application, I included everything I could think of: yard work and house maintenance, farming, and of course, basic mechanics and auto body repair.

Cil's parents had no phone so I would check twice a week for messages at the Jensens or the Burdens or the Surkans, who lived nearby. That way, I could visit with the neighbours as well as keep up with anything important coming from the employment office. I made the odd phone call to the local auto body shops, hoping there might be an opening for an apprenticeship trainee position. Jerry was apprenticing at the Hilltop Wreckers and Auto Body Shop.

One day a friend of the Gregoires, Ed Smith, came to visit and we got talking about rebuilding cars. I told him about my experience in Kelowna through the technical school.

"So, you've got some experience taking out motors and rebuilding them?"

"Yeah, I rebuilt a 1955 Ford four-door from scratch."

"How would you like to work with me? I've got this small job. It's only paying $200 plus parts. The lady wants her car running by spring."

"Sure! When do we start?"

The motor had seized under pressure. Stripping it was a piece of cake, but putting the new parts in and replacing the engine was tough. We didn't have the necessary tools to line everything up, so it was a struggle getting everything to its original state. At times, the job was tedious. We were working outside in the cold in a lean-to garage with the car sitting on blocks high enough to work under, using a tripod to hoist the engine. But I learned more about engines and parts in that two weeks than I did in five months at the college. Ed was no mechanic; anytime he got stuck he'd flip through the pages of the fix-it manual he packed with him. He knew enough to rebuild the motor and have it purring like a kitten.

As the month of March approached, the weather was beginning to change. The days became clearer. Everywhere the snow was melting and puddles made the ground muddy.

I was becoming anxious, looking forward to my twenty-first birthday on March 15. This birthday was important. It would bring me privileges such as the right to vote, to purchase liquor and enter licensed premises, to sign documents for myself, and specifically, to get my driver's licence. Jerry, Willard, and Perry were all older than me by at least nine months, so I was the one sitting outside in the car while they had their beer and played pool.

At this same time, I received a welcome surprise. Cil told me she was pregnant. We were both happy at the thought; I was very excited that I was going to be a father. The reality of a baby confirmed my conviction to return home to Creston. I rubbed Cil's stomach. "We need to give this baby a place to live. He's going to get everything I ever had and more."

"How do you know it's a he?" she asked.

"I just have a feeling."

I knew deep inside and Cil did, too, that we needed to raise this child in an environment that wasn't so complex. I thought of all the things I had done in my youth, and how I could simplify the traditional aspects of raising our own child.

On the first of April, after my wife played the April Fool joke I always fell for ("Jerry's here! Get out of bed!"), I decided to actually find Jerry and ask him to take me into Vernon. I wanted to check in at the employment centre.

Jerry was great about driving me where I wanted to go. We parked in front of the Post Office, and I ran upstairs to check the information board and to talk with the employment officer. She mentioned that a potato farmer needed someone with experience driving tractor to disk and harrow several fields and do some work in the potato shed.

"I'm interested," I said, "but I've never worked with potatoes before. I'll give it a try."

"I'll call him right now for a start date."

While I waited, I was worried about Jerry sitting downstairs in the car. Patience was not one of his strengths. He was slow doing things, but when he needed to do something, it was right now.

The woman hung up the phone. "The farmer's name is Fred Becktoldt and he lives out on Grandview Flats. He'll pick you up here at ten o'clock on Tuesday. I told him about your farming experience."

"I'll be here," I said, feeling excited about the news.

"What took you so long?" asked Jerry, when I finally jumped back in the car.

"I got a job with a farmer! I have to be here on Tuesday, so I need a ride in."

"Good man," my friend said. "No problem. I'll drive you."

We drove north along the Old Kamloops Highway towards Head-of-the-Lake. I noticed there was no snow left in the fields. Jerry was quiet for a long time, and I could tell he was deep in thought, that something was bothering him.

"What's wrong, partner?" I asked.

"When I was waiting for you, I started thinking about all the fun times we've had, even back to the days at the residential school and before you got married, and even now. It's going to be hard to say goodbye."

"Yeah, it's going to be hard. But you know it's not a forever thing; I'll be travelling back here to visit as often as I can. Cil's roots are here and our children will need to visit their grandparents because they don't have any back home. Hey, man, you know I can get work much easier in Creston. Look at all the times I've gone into Vernon to try and find a job. I know people at home who will give me work."

As we passed the O'Keefe Ranch, which had become a historical site in 1967, we were quiet again. We turned onto Head-of-the-Lake Road and into the Gregoire driveway so I could share my good news.

The Becktoldt potato farm was less than a mile away from Cecilia's dad's property, on the other side of the railroad tracks and up the hill. It seemed that Tuesday was taking forever to arrive. I was anxious about the job, what I would be doing, and what it would be like working for Fred.

When I left the house with Jerry that first morning, I grabbed my lunch and gave Cil a kiss. "I guess I'm about as ready for work as I'll ever be."

"Remember to cut across the field after work," said Cil.

The drive to Vernon was quiet until Jerry commented, "Guess no practice tonight. You'll be too tired."

"Come and see me after six, and we'll work something out," I said.

We were twenty minutes early at the employment office. "Jerry, does this remind you of us in Kelowna?"

He looked at me questioningly. "What do you mean, Luke?"

"Well, remember I would practically drag you to school some mornings, and sometimes I would leave without you. I think that somewhere, somehow, you finally got the idea that being early for some things pays off."

"Yeah, you're right, it does feel good to be early, but it makes the day seem long."

I only waited ten minutes for Fred Becktoldt to arrive. He was stocky, about my height, in his mid-thirties. He was clean-shaven and had short hair.

"You must be Chris Luke," he said, shaking my hand. "I'm

the potato farmer." He looked at me from head to foot. "Ready for some hard work, are you?"

"Nothing I can't handle," I answered.

On our way to the car, he questioned me. "What more can you tell me about what you've done besides cutting and hauling hay?"

"I've done some cultivating and a bit of harrowing, preparing the land for seeding. That's about it for tractor work."

We got into Fred's red and white pickup, a 1968 Ford half-ton F-100 series, and drove north. Just past the O'Keefe Ranch, we turned onto St. Anne's Hill Road.

"I'm renting this property from a neighbour. I'll show you where you'll be working, and then we'll get you some gloves from the farm and I can check in for messages."

I took note of the thirty-acre field, the red Massey-Ferguson tractor with the set of disks attached, and the harrows on a twenty-four-foot bar sitting next to the fence line.

Fred found me a nice-fitting pair of leather gloves, which he said I could keep, and we headed back to the field. "I want you to disk this and then switch to the harrows. When you're done, just unhook everything and drive the tractor back to the farm. Okay? I don't expect you to finish this today." He jumped back into his truck and left.

He hadn't told me what he was going to plant, but I presumed it would be either grass or alfalfa. I began disking north/south and then east/west, and harrowed from the northeast to the southwest corner of the property. It took me the better part of two days to complete the field. When Fred came to inspect my work of art, he was impressed.

"Where did you learn to drive tractor and all?" he asked.

"After my fourteenth birthday, when school was out in the summer, I helped my dad. He worked with one of the leading ranchers in Creston Valley who owned about three hundred and fifty head of cattle. I learned on the tractor when Dad was helping to break ground and plant alfalfa."

I did some more work on a smaller section close to Fred's farm. During the third week of April, I started work in the packing shed. My job was to dump sacks of seed potatoes onto a conveyor belt so four women could cut them up. The belt then carried the quartered potatoes to drop into cups that then emptied into sacks. I would tie the filled sacks and replace them with empties. I moved the finished potatoes to a separate pile on a dolly that accommodated four sacks at a time. After that, a truck hauled them to the field for planting.

I noticed that the seed potatoes came from the Wynndel packing shed. "Is Wynndel the only place you deal with for seed potatoes?" I asked Fred.

"Yeah, they're a very reasonable price, even with the cost of transportation."

I felt a bit of pride, knowing what I was handling came from the Creston Valley. I also enjoyed working for Fred for those fourteen days. He certainly was an easygoing guy. I told him I was returning to Creston with my bride and expected baby.

"I hate to see you leave, Chris. You're a great worker. You've got a lot of patience and people love having you around. All the ladies spoke highly of you—they said you kept them busy."

I had worked one hundred and twelve hours at $1.25 per

hour, which gave me $140. Fred also added a bonus of $20. "Thanks for being available," he said.

I was ecstatic. I ran down the hill, across the tracks, and onto my father-in-law's property. I ran until I got to the house, told Cecilia the good news, and still had lots of energy to hitchhike to Jerry's to get him to take us all to town for a celebration supper at the Lotus Gardens.

As the weather improved, Cecilia and I would take walks toward Round Lake and back, often with one or two of her brothers and sisters. It was two miles to the end of the public road and another one thousand metres to the lake. Round Lake has a healing effect about it and, as such, it is sacred. Today, the Round Lake Native Treatment Centre is a place of physical, emotional, and spiritual rejuvenation for people who suffer from substance abuse.

In the winter of 1967, when we first knew each other, ice had formed on the lake, probably four or five inches thick. I would run and slide on the surface, which made Cil laugh; the more I tried to run as I slipped around, the more she would laugh. We were warned about cougars in the area, but like most teenagers who are in love or think they are in love, nothing else mattered to us.

These walks became special, because usually we talked about important things, decisions we had to make. One May morning, we headed toward Round Lake Road and talked about what we would be leaving behind and the uncertainty about living in Creston. Cil was concerned about being pregnant and having no one in her family with her when the child was born. I hadn't thought about it, but she did have a point. Traditionally, grandparents play a large role with the first-born of their children.

I knew there was no one in Creston we could really count on for support, guidance, and protection. There certainly wasn't anybody back home I could place my faith and trust in. Would we survive the disadvantages and adversities that people in most Native communities were facing?

She remained unsure, and I became stubborn. I didn't want to listen. Usually our disagreements could be resolved, but this was one of the rare times when our discussion ended up in an argument. We both had to have the last say, and we both had to be right.

Neither of us was gaining any headway. My stubbornness took hold. I told her I was leaving for good. I packed my things, stuffing my suitcase as full as I could. As I was going out the door, I said to her, "See you sometime...I'll write you."

She looked up at me. "Don't bother."

I wasn't getting any sympathy whatsoever from her. Something told me I could not back down and give in to her. I had to carry through with my plan to leave. I started walking down the road to the main highway, thinking I would go to Jerry's, stay overnight, and catch the bus home to Creston the next day. Just before the highway started its descent to the valley floor, a highway patrol car stopped; the officer called me over.

"Where are you going with your suitcase?" he asked. "What's your name? Where are you from?"

I answered him, and he asked if I had any tattoos or markings. I guessed that the police were looking for someone with a certain type of mark on his body. I showed him my right forearm, where I had inscribed a homemade tattoo when I was eleven years old. I used India ink and a heated needle on the end of a pencil to write *CRESTON* and my initials, *C.L.* The officer looked at it, thanked me, and said, "Good luck," to end the interrogation. "I hope you make your destination."

I looked back toward the house one more time. Someone was crossing the railroad tracks and walking in my direction, so I waited. It was Cecilia. We stood facing each other.

"What do you want?" I asked.

"This was not my idea. Mom told me I should come after you…and I don't really want you to go."

"I really didn't want to go either," I said and reached out to grab her. We hugged for a long while, tears running down our faces. We knew then how much we cared for each other. But we were finding out that marriage certainly had its ups and downs.

On the way back to the house, we aired our concerns about Creston once more. I reassured Cecilia, "If things don't work out back home, we'll just move back here."

That day we drove to Vernon with Jerry to have lunch at King's Café and to buy our bus tickets. They cost $16.65 each. As I stuffed them in my shirt pocket, I smiled at Cil, took her hand, and said jokingly, "Our tickets to paradise. I feel almost the way I did when we left to go south to Kelso, but this is special. I am going home with you by my side, and you are going to have a baby." We would leave the next week on Thursday at 11:25 a.m.

It was a very emotional time for us—especially for Cecilia. She still mentions that she never really had the opportunity to say goodbye properly to her parents, her friends, the home she grew up in, the Okanagan Valley—her roots.

As First Nations people born into a traditional family, we have a responsibility, an obligation to the land and its resources. The land does not belong to us, we belong to it; we must protect the land, while utilizing what we need. I often think that I need to repay my wife for her sacrifice. I need to spend time with her on her land.

That weekend, Inqualla put on a dance as a going-away gift to us. Jerry had made up three notices and posted them. We charged $3 per person at the door. The proceeds would be ours for our trip and for food once we got to Creston.

This last dance was emotional for me, a heart-warming experience. The floor was packed because word of "Luke's farewell dance party" had spread like wildfire. I was on a real high. I sang all our songs with a lot of feeling. After the first set, I announced that this was my final performance with the group, that I was taking my bride and returning to my own village of Yaqan Nukiy. We continued to offer our old stand-bys and also played a couple of new tunes we had been practising: "Purple Haze" by Jimi Hendrix and "Proud Mary" by Creedence Clearwater Revival. We tried to wrap the dance up by one-thirty a.m., but the crowd wanted more. I announced we would play for another hour and that we would be passing the hat. "Don't be shy," I said. "Throw in $5 to make it worthwhile!"

Luckily it wasn't an all-nighter, although the crowd kept chanting, "More! More! More!" By three in the morning, my voice was beginning to break, so I made my final announcement. With the admission price and cash from the hat, we made $500, which I knew would come in handy as Cil and I began our journey. I gave each of the guys some of the cash because they earned it.

The next Thursday arrived. We had done our packing—two big boxes and two suitcases. We sat at the table eating our usual eggs and toast and sipping our coffee. Cecilia's sisters and brothers were leaving for school. They were crying as she said goodbye to each of them in turn. "Do you really have to go?" they asked.

"Yes, I want to be with Chris. But I promise you we'll visit once we get settled into our own place."

I tried to comfort her as we waited on the porch in the sunshine for Jerry to arrive. "I wish we could stay, but we have no future here. At home, there will be work right away because I know people."

Jerry pulled up in his Victoria Crown around ten o'clock. "Ready to go, Luke?" he yelled, with a big smile on his face.

"We've been ready for awhile," I answered.

As we packed our stuff into the trunk, Jerry said, "I'm supposed to tell you that everyone at Head-of-the-Lake says to have a safe trip home and look after each other. If things don't work out, they said to remember you've got a place in Vernon."

Cil's mom and dad shed a few tears as we said our good-byes. Cil couldn't keep from crying either. Edna said, "If things are too much for you, if you're lonesome, come home for a while."

We drove onto Turner Road, with Jerry beeping the horn all the way down the drive until we were out of sight. He didn't linger at the bus depot. He said he wanted to get home right away and mumbled something about having a problem with saying goodbye. I sat across from Cil in the bus depot café sipping Coke and watching tears well up in her eyes and slowly run down her cheeks.

It was perfect travelling weather—not a cloud in the sky. We sat on the left side of the bus so we could view the lakes as we headed south. We stopped in Winfield for five minutes, then Westbank, Peachland, Summerland, and Penticton, where we had to wait two and a half hours before transferring to another bus.

We stored our luggage in a large bin inside the depot and found a restaurant. While we were eating, I shared some of the things I was looking forward to at home.

"Hunting the spring bucks, gathering duck eggs, watching the annual spring flood. When it floods, it looks like a huge lake in behind the village to the west. We even go swimming and boating as long as we can until the water goes down in July. I can't wait to walk along the hills towards Porthill, Idaho…I'll show you all the places I've gone hunting and trapping and hiking."

Cil loves reading so we looked for a book for the trip. When the bus from Vancouver pulled in, we watched the passengers who got out to stretch their legs or get something to eat or use the washroom. There were no toilets on buses in the 1960s.

We left on schedule, 4:20 p.m. There were stops in Okanagan Falls, Oliver, and Osoyoos, a supper stop of forty-five minutes in Grand Forks before we rumbled on to Castlegar and Nelson. The final stretch was over the two-year-old Salmo-Creston highway through Kootenay Pass. The driver told us we would arrive in Creston before midnight. Heading up the west side of the summit took most of the time, but once we reached the top and the east side, we were cruising.

"This is a beautiful drive in the daytime," I told Cil. "The scenery is excellent, except where the forest fire burned the mountain." We both agreed we would save our money to buy a car and make a trip over the Salmo-Creston while the weather remained nice.

The bus rolled across the Creston flats and turned onto Highway 21. Excitement ran through me as we reached Canyon Street and passed the elevators, Godfrey's Motor Inn, the Club Cafe, the pool hall, Avery-Carr Pharmacy, and the red brick Canadian Imperial Bank of Commerce.

Gordon Gardner, owner and driver of the taxi business, was waiting for a fare at the depot and was very helpful in gathering our things and driving us to the Lower Kootenay Community. He was curious, probably because he hadn't seen me before. Who was I? Where did I live? How long had I been gone? What was I doing away from Creston? What was I planning to do back here?

The village was dark so Gordon shone the car lights toward the family house so we could unload our stuff. I must have knocked on the door for several minutes before Mary opened it. She was definitely caught off guard. "How come you didn't write to let us know you were coming home?"

"We wanted to surprise everyone."

Mary said she would talk to us in the morning and went back to bed. We dug into our boxes for sheets and blankets. As we warmed up to each other, Cil asked, "So what are your plans for tomorrow?"

"After breakfast, we can visit with Mary, and then I'll introduce you to everyone in the village."

We lay in the dark talking and thinking about the future. I was worried about my resume and my lack of references. All I knew was that I needed work. I didn't want to disappoint Cecilia or myself.

14

FITTING IN

WHEN I WOKE UP THE NEXT MORNING, MY BROTHER Rudy was already gone from the house. He was off helping Ike Basil and Frank Francis (Frenchie) build a float for the upcoming Creston Blossom Festival.

"There's coffee made," said Mary, "and help yourself to eggs and sausages in the fridge in the back room."

"So, what's new? What's happening around here?" I asked.

"There are three new homes—Zachary Basil, Isobel Louie, and Theresa Pierre—and another three coming up this summer for Stanley White and Ike Basil, and one of them is for me."

"Is it for you personally, or is it to replace the family home? What's the deal, because I would like to live here in the old house if the new house is just for you."

"They're talking about tearing down this house once we move into the new one," Mary said.

"Well, I guess that means we have to move also."

"It's not going to be ready until later this year, late fall," she said.

"Good. No sense getting all worked up right now."

Cil and I ate breakfast and I headed out for a shower. At that time, Lower Kootenay had a community laundry, showers, and bath all in one building situated to the rear of the hall. On some days it was the busiest place in the village. There was no indoor plumbing in the community; everyone had an outhouse. Each house had running water, but to get hot water, we heated it on the stove.

Cil and I checked out the float construction. We could hear sawing, hammering, and a lot of laughter coming from the south side of the house. Rudy, Ike, and Frenchie were repairing the flat deck trailer for the float. While we were talking with them, Zachary Basil came by on his way to check the basement that had been dug recently by the church. He greeted me, asked how I was doing, and said to George Kusiak, the housing contractor, "Has he got into any trouble yet?" Zach was now the Band manager. He and George were putting up the forms to pour cement the following week. The backhoe was operated by Richard Dewald, whom I would later play with in the band known as Dewalds' Orchestra. He was an excellent guitar player.

The Band Council of the time consisted of Chief Isaac Basil and Councillors Mary Basil and Stanley White. The Department of Indian Affairs was finally fulfilling its fiduciary obligations in assisting the Band with new homes. As I understood it, the Band had entered into a five-year lease agreement with the Federal Government to build new homes in exchange for wetlands to be utilized by the Canadian Wildlife Service and Ducks Unlimited (Canada). In essence, the homes being built were paid for out of funds received through this lease agreement; they were not "free" homes, as

Summer 1969—Cil and I when we first moved back to Creston, B.C., Yaqan Nukiy Village.

speculated by John Doe, Joe Blow, and Jane Dick. It was enlightening to know that, after years and years of living in matchboxes, we were actually getting new modest housing. Now in 1969 we were going to enjoy indoor plumbing, hot water tanks, bathtubs, and electrical appliances.

Cil and I made the rounds that morning. We visited my sister Cecile, Aunt Nancy, Isobel, Adrian, Irene, Florine, and Christine. Robert and Joan were both at school. Freddy, Wayne, and Carol Louie were all living away from Creston in foster homes. We visited my sister Doreen, her husband Pete, and their nine-month-old son, Larry. Doreen was so happy to see us, she hugged us for the longest time. Over coffee, we discussed what had happened since they returned from Washington, and I asked about work. Pete said he had applied to clear right-of-way for a pipeline and that he would find out about the job in a week.

"Zachary mentioned putting some guys to work so they could earn a few dollars for Blossom Festival," I said.

"Work where?" Pete asked.

"Fencing on the north boundary of the reserve. It's supposed to take about a week. It sounds like he's putting me in charge of the crew. Anyway, if you're not doing any clearing by the time we start fencing, I'll be calling on you."

"Okay," said Pete.

"Zach also told me that once the housing project gets into full swing, I could get hired on as a carpenter's helper."

On the way home, Cil and I stopped by the new basement. Stanley White, nicknamed Skeezix, was helping with the forms. I found out he and his wife, Irene Isadore, had another son born in November.

I noticed that our old home, the one that was converted into a shed and storage place, had been torn down. I asked Mary about it.

"What happened to all the equipment and tools, harnesses and saddles that were stored there?"

She hesitated and started to explain what she had done. "I sold the horses, harnesses, and wagon to a lady named Ibbitson," she said.

I believe that here began my frustration and lack of trust with my sister. I had come home to nothing. I'd had plans for the horses and equipment. Not one penny had been sent to me, nor did I receive any acknowledgement of the decisions made regarding Dad's belongings. Mary had sold all the things that were so special in my mind. She even sold my mother's buckskin dress and dancing regalia. I thought my parents' things ought to have been kept by a family member and handed down through the generations. I have not yet gone past this frustration.

As the first day at home wore on, I was not feeling as positive. I wandered around the village with Rudy and checked out the black soil that had been exposed when the foundations were removed from the old homes. At least here was something I could begin with.

"This is it, Rudy. I can grow a garden right here. It just needs tilling."

The following day, Cil and I hiked to town. We needed to check the mail, buy some seeds, and get some gas for Stanley's rototiller. I also wanted to leave some job applications with the auto body shops. There were two shops that I was aware of—Richter Auto Body and Dominion Paint & Body Service. I knew both owners, Ed Richter and Ed Gatzke. Both of them were easygoing people. You could strike up a conversation with them and actually hold their attention.

Ed Richter stood five feet nine inches tall and weighed approximately 185 pounds. He wore a crewcut and smile. He still wears a crewcut today, and he hasn't lost his smile. He wanted to know more about me personally, how I managed to get away to finish grade ten and complete the automotive training program.

"There was a lot at stake," I said. "I promised my dad I would finish school. He wanted me to become an auto mechanic because he thought I could make a lot of money to support a family." I didn't tell him that I probably wouldn't have completed the course without the encouragement of Brenda's family and Mr. and Mrs. Bob Comfort, especially as Dad had passed away.

I talked with Ed about the circumstances of reservation life. Looking back at my life then from today's point of view, I would have thought there was no future for me. I needed to get away and build a whole new life elsewhere. Ed seemed to understand; he seemed to care about my plans. He actually wanted me to succeed and achieve my goals. I told him that I really wanted to finish my apprenticeship in the auto body trade and build my own business on the reservation.

After that conversation with Ed, I had a good feeling that he would be calling on me to work for him.

Cil and I headed to Sinclair's Hardware to buy seeds and a jerry can for gas. I knew the proprietor, George Sinclair, and got along well with him. His daughter Peggy, my sister Doreen, and Gordon Armstrong's daughter Rae were all born about the same time. My mother had done her shopping at Sinclair's and I carried on the tradition. We headed for the Garden Bakery, where my mother had bought bread, meat pies, and pastries. We still buy bakery items there. After lunch at the Club Cafe, we continued to the Shell station to buy gas for the rototiller.

Within a couple of days, I had the garden tilled and planted and fenced by recycling old wire and posts with staples in them. Soon, I was in charge of replacing posts and repairing fence along the northern portion of the reserve property next to the Goat River, which was leased out for grazing purposes. After work each day, I would check the garden, pull weeds, and water it.

It took Pete, Steve Pierre, Moses George, Frenchie, and myself three weeks to finish the fence line and move on to the east fence line adjacent to Riverview and Buterman Road to the south. Having worked with my father and then with Jerry and his dad, I had a lot of experience fencing. I drove the guys around in a beat-up pickup, cutting down the smaller cedar trees for fence posts, replacing or reversing the original posts, depending on their condition. Zach had set us up behind and above the community to cut the posts. By the fourth day of cutting and splitting the logs, we had more than two hundred posts. We were able to stockpile some for future repairs to the south and west portions of the reserve and for Reserves 1B, 1C, 2, 3, 4, and 5.

All this time, we were anticipating Blossom Festival weekend. It brought back special memories. My father, mother, uncles, aunts, and other members of the community participated in the annual parade. My mother and father dressed in their regalia. Uncle Louis Ernest rode his horses and Uncle Gabe, Aunt Margaret, and other band members walked behind. In 1960, my sister Doreen and I rode on a float with George Oliver's son, while Mom and Dad rode their horses. I realize now that riding in the parade was next to being a tradition that my parents took very seriously.

So it was nice to know that the Lower Kootenay Band was putting a float into the parade again. Rudy, Ike, and Frenchie were working on it steadily.

As it turned out, the parade that year was excellent. It started at the Adam Robertson Elementary School grounds and proceeded through town to the Prince Charles Secondary School grounds. Ike and Frenchie both sat on the float in front of a teepee with the Kootenay Canoe beside them, with trees, a fire pit, drying and tanning racks propped up next to the teepee—a nice setup. Robert Louie drove the tractor that pulled the float. Robert told me later that the reason Ike and Frenchie would disappear into the teepee was that they were taking turns sipping away at a bottle of whiskey they had stashed. "Did you notice," asked Robert, "how shit-faced they looked smiling and waving away at the people?"

At the end of the parade route, Robert asked them to get off because he wanted to return the tractor and trailer to the owner. Frenchie wouldn't get down, so Robert had to grab him and drag him off. He left him there on the ground because Frenchie was so drunk he couldn't move.

Cil and I actually had a good time at the festival that weekend. We took in the fastball tournament, the mini-rodeo in Canyon, and the amusement rides on the high school field. The Lower Kootenay Band was not yet hosting an annual powwow.

The month of June was upon us and everything was in full bloom, especially my garden. The corn, potatoes, radishes, onions, and cucumbers were breaking through the ground and the tomato plants were already flowering. I weeded every chance I had and kept busy doing odd jobs for the Band. Zach had a list of things he wanted done, and one of them was painting the three new homes. Frenchie and I were given contracts to do the painting, so much per home. The people who would live there selected the colours and I went along to pick up the supplies. I painted Zach and Mary Basil's residence, and Frenchie painted the Louie home. Once finished, we were going to paint the Pierre house together. I completed two coats on the Basil home, while Frenchie finished his first coat and then went on a binge.

As it turned out, I ended up painting the second coat on the Louie residence and working on the Pierre home by myself. I started with two coats on the gable ends, doorframes, and house trim, then painted the major part of the house and immediately gave it its second coat. While I was painting the north end, I fell off the scaffolding and landed on my back. Luckily, I didn't break any bones, but I was badly bruised. I fell about sixteen feet from the peak of the gable end. Today I'm somewhat afraid of heights. I feel nauseated anytime I look out the window of a hotel room in Vancouver. In that two weeks I made $450, which helped me forget my accident. But I haven't painted any more houses.

Zach asked if I was ready to work as a carpenter's helper. He said that George Kusiak was a hard worker and expected an honest day's work from anyone who worked with him. I began to work immediately nailing down shingles on the roof of Stanley White's house. The job consisted of measuring and chalking up three lines spaced out evenly, and tacking down the shingles beginning from the bottom and middle of the roof on up with the first layer of shingles upside down.

I also liked to work with the Skilsaw, cutting 2x4s to

length. George Kusiak had a special contraption that would cut 2x4s in eight-foot lengths for studding. I spent time building trusses for a couple of the new homes. I began hammering studs for the outside walls and for the partitions separating the hallways and bedrooms.

The work wasn't what I had expected. I actually enjoyed working on the Lower Kootenay Band housing project. I was learning about carpentry and how important accurate measurements were in the construction of a house. I wanted to learn as much as I could about building.

Working for the Band was like a mirror of events. It reflected that what I was doing was actually what I had dreamed of doing when I was still a kid. The men in the community were working either at building, renovating, or putting additions on some of the older homes. Waterlines were being repaired or changed over, and digging was very much part of that. I used to tell myself that was what I wanted to be doing someday, and here I was home again and working for the Band.

I looked forward to each and every day when I got up in the morning. Cil and I would have a chat over breakfast before I went off to work. She was beginning to show her pregnancy, being in the fifth month. Any time we talked about the baby, I would say "he," "the boy," "our boy," or "our son." Cil would always ask, "How do you know it's a boy?" And I would answer, "I just know!"

One morning, we sat sipping our coffee, talking about our good fortune. "You're lucky you're working," Cil said. "I need to tell you that you were right when you said you could find work here right away."

Having her acknowledgement reassured me that work was

endless, and it depended on a person's work ethic. Zach, George, Ike, and Stan appreciated my performance. They all knew they could depend on me to be on time, to be ready to work with very little supervision, to finish whatever I was doing, and to stay after the end of the day to make sure everything was put away.

I knew the job with the Band was going to end in November, and I certainly didn't want to be sitting around after that. I wanted a full-time job, and the way Rudy and I started working for the J.H. Huscroft sawmill was a godsend.

While tacking down the last two rows of shingles on Stanley's roof, I noticed Zach talking with two people parked in front of his house. I recognized them as George and Don Kepke, both of whom lived on Highway 21 just up the road from the reserve. They walked over and stood at the bottom of the ladder looking up at us.

"Come down for a minute, Chris," said Zach.

All sorts of thoughts went through my head. Maybe they wanted me to mend fence for them, do some carpentry, haul hay. I didn't know what to expect. As I reached the ground, both George and Don had their hands out to greet me.

George spoke first. "Well, Chris, Don and I both work for Huscrofts, and we're recruiting people to work at the mill. Ken, the owner, suggested we find someone here in the band who might be interested."

I only had one question. "Is it steady employment?"

George and Don looked at each other. "Yeah, we were told it was permanent."

I was getting excited. "Sure! I'm interested. When does the job start?"

"Do you know anyone else who wants to work?" asked Don.

"My brother Rudy would be a good worker," I said.

"What you and your brother need to do in the next day or so is go to the mill and fill out some papers. They'll tell you when you can start work."

After they left, George Kusiak told us to take a coffee break before we moved on to Mary's house. I ran home, where Cil had just made a pitcher of lemonade. I told her my good news, but Rudy wasn't home.

The Monday after that, George, Stanley, Ike, and I moved our tools to Mary's new house on the north side of the church. All it had at this point was a basement and main floor with an opening for the basement door. The main floor was marked with chalk to indicate where the outside walls and partitions were supposed to go. By lunchtime we had all the walls up and were plating the partitions. All the headers were in place, windows and doorways, closets, and chimney space. By afternoon coffee break, we had almost finished nailing the trusses together to begin placing the rafters. George had already told me I could be excused to fill out my application at the mill.

Rudy was waiting for me, and we drove to Erickson. The secretary at the mill knew immediately what we wanted. After we had filled out the applications, we had an interview with Ken Huscroft. He asked about our work background. I did most of the answering to take attention away from Rudy, who had very little work experience. Rudy told me later he was nervous because he didn't have any idea about what he would be doing at the mill. Two weeks later we got a call that we were to start work on the last Monday of July 1969 at seven in the morning.

We pulled into the mill parking lot where the crew were arriving, taking their lunch boxes to the lunch room. I recognized some of the workers: Geordie Phypers, Roger Huscroft, John Kriese, George Huscroft, Bill Huscroft, Jim and Joe Moman, Les Tooze and, of course, George and Don Kepke. I was no stranger to them, either. I introduced Rudy and in turn I was introduced to Ozzie Spagis and Joe Giella, who worked on the green chain where I was assigned.

The green chain is a conveyer belt that carries wood from the edger to a drop sorter that further moves the boards into separate piles; for example, all the one-inch material is placed on one side and the two-inch material on the other. The length of the boards could be from eight feet to twelve feet.

Ozzie was very friendly and we got along well. At first, he asked me a lot of questions. Had I lived in the valley all my life? Was I with someone? How long had I been married? He told me about his own unique background (he was a Lapp, of the reindeer people). He filled me in about work, about shutdowns, emergencies, work breaks—all the things I needed to know.

I often spoke with George Huscroft, who ran the edger. We had a lot in common, especially hunting. He was one of those people who didn't worry about giving you a piece of his mind. He would say to me, "Chris, you don't want to work here for the rest of your life, do you?" And I would answer, "Of course not!" And he would ask, "So what are you going to do?" "Well, I'm going to be chief someday." I cherish those moments when I realize I have earned respect from those I worked with. Today whenever we run into each other, George smiles and says, "So, you're still the chief…"

Joe Giella was a hard worker. Every once in a while when the material would plug up on his side, he'd holler at Ozzie and me to give him a hand. Sometimes we'd pretend we didn't hear him; other times we would start clapping. Ozzie told me that Joe was always so serious and that he'd been trying to soften him up and make him smile.

Ozzie and I patrolled our side of the green chain like a pair of border patrol guards. The minute a board dropped, it was in the pile right away. Rudy worked in the main building; his job was to remove rocks from the logs, wash them, and feed the head saw a log at a time.

When George Huscroft took a week's holiday for hunting elk, Ozzie, Joe, and I took turns tailing the edger; John Kriese, who usually did the tailing, fed the edger. When George returned to work, there was a spike bull rack mounted on the crash bar at the front of his truck. He told us the animal he got dressed out well over three hundred pounds.

All in all, I didn't mind the work at the mill, but I hated the standing time when no logs were coming through or there was a breakdown. Knowing I would be working steady prompted Cil and I to apply for a telephone, which was installed within a couple of weeks. We still have the same telephone number today.

15

FIRST CAR

NOW THAT I HAD SOME MONEY COMING IN, CIL AND I were saving up for a car. I also wanted a 30-30 rifle, as I was still using a .22 single-shot to hunt with.

I was seriously considering getting my driver's licence, but I was unsure of the timing because I didn't have much experience driving around. Zach Basil told me I could borrow his car when I was ready to take my road test. He drove a 1961 Pontiac Parisienne four-door sedan, an automatic with a six-cylinder motor that was in prime condition.

Cil and I opened a savings account at the Royal Bank on Canyon Street and deposited what money we had when we arrived from Vernon and the money I was earning working for the Band. Eventually, we wanted to save enough to buy a vehicle and a rifle.

My dad had owned a 30-30 Winchester Model 94 that had been handed down from his grandfather and father. I loved that rifle; I shot my second deer with it. When I asked my sister Mary what had happened to it, she said she had sold it to Mr. Charlie Whitford as an antique after I left for the

Okanagan. Hunting was important to me, and I wondered why she hadn't thought of giving it to me. It was still useful; it wasn't an antique.

George Sinclair at the hardware store told me there was a sale on 30-30 Model 94 rifles. He had ordered a dozen and I bought one. It cost me $107 with tax.

I passed the driver's written exam, with one incorrect answer. The question was to do with parking downhill, either into or away from the curb, when there is no curb. I borrowed Zach's car several times to practise driving so I could take the road test, but Cil suggested we look around for a vehicle we could afford. Then we could insure it and find someone with a driver's licence who could ride with us while I got more experience handling the car.

Zach called on me one evening. Did I want to check on a car with him? The vehicle was in excellent shape—a '62 four-door Chevrolet, six-cylinder—but the price that Bruce Richter wanted was definitely out of my price range.

One weekend in July, Cil and I hiked to town to check out the car lots. The first place we checked was the GM dealership owned by Ray Schmalz. His business operated out of what is now Pharmasave. The offices were up front and a two-bay garage was at the back; the car lot was located behind McDowells' store, the area that now houses the Creston Valley Advance, accountant, and law offices. Then we walked up the street to George Nedelec's Kootenay Lake Motors (Ford and Mercury) whose offices were in the present B.C. Government

Agent's building. The garage area in the back is now occupied by Lorne Mann's notary office. Nedelec's car lot was behind the Rendezvous Restaurant, which at that time was the bus depot.

Further up the street was Creston Valley Automotive, owned and operated by Al Ingham. He ran the Chrysler Dodge offices and New Holland Massey-Ferguson farm equipment departments across from the automotive section, which was in the Sun R building, with the car lot located on the former Bank of Montreal site.

Cil and I spent most of the afternoon checking out vehicles. We found one car in each lot that we thought we could afford, but being newly married and pinching pennies, we decided we should hold off for a while longer.

Because we had a healthy savings account with the Royal Bank, I thought there wouldn't be a problem getting a loan with them. What happened wasn't what I expected.

The loans officer, whom I knew (or thought I knew), told me flat out that they didn't give loans to Indian people. I was shocked, outraged, humiliated. It brought back memories of my earlier years going to school. I had non-Native friends who did not deal with banks, yet received substantial loans— much more money than what I was requesting. I wanted to withdraw all our savings and march up the street to the Canadian Imperial Bank of Commerce, but decided against it. I did not want to face further humiliation.

I left the bank. "What happened?" asked Cil, who had seen that look of anger and rejection on my face many times before.

"I'm a f— Indian, and they can't get past the colour."

She suggested I should cool off, go sit in the Club Cafe and have a Coke. "Good idea," I said. "At least Mah Toy won't refuse us service."

I shared my bank experience with Zach, who asserted that Creston was eighty per cent racist. I was in shock because I was used to people being more friendly, as they had been in Vernon. (I did not ask the bank for anything for two years. When I needed money for another vehicle, my status had obviously changed, because they gave me a loan.)

Zach was looking to purchase a station wagon but didn't know if he should sell his Pontiac outright or use it as a trade-in. "We'll buy it, if the price is right," I said.

Eventually, we did buy Zach's car for $350 and insured it. After that, there wasn't a weekend that we stayed at home. I drove the car everywhere and wherever we went, Robert Louie was with us. We drove down to Kootenay Lake, across on the ferry to Nelson, Castlegar, and Trail, and back over the Salmo-Creston summit. I was getting in all the driving experience that I could. We even took trips to Cranbrook to visit Joe and Sophie Pierre, who had been married one year before Cil and I. I was surprised that their car was the same make and the same year as ours, except that it only had two doors.

Finally, I took my road test and passed without any difficulty. The tester was impressed with my driving skills. At the Government Agent's office, then located in the present Town Hall building, I signed for my new licence.

I was glad I hadn't jeopardized my chances of getting that licence the week before when I was driving to the mill. Rudy was with me. As we drove up the back road, we could see a police roadblock at Erickson and 25th Avenue. What to do? I

1969—A proud and happy moment. We had just bought our first car, a 1961 Pontiac 4-door sedan.

owned the car, it was insured to the max, I was twenty-one, but I only had a learner's licence.

We stopped at the Mohawk station, bought a bit of gas, and decided to drive up 20th to Canyon Street and then east to 33rd and around to the mill that way. Some of the guys mentioned being pulled over; the RCMP were checking for registration and licences and looking at vehicles for safety purposes.

"Did you get stopped, Chris?" someone asked.

I looked over at Rudy. I wasn't going to risk my licence by being honest. "No, we drove around through town," I said.

16

FIRST-BORN

CIL WAS DUE TO GIVE BIRTH WITHIN THE NEXT MONTH, and I was getting more excited as each day went by.

Ozzie would constantly bombard me with questions. "When is the baby due? How do you know it's a boy? Why do you want to name him after yourself?"

The two of us spent weekends at the mill loading railroad ties into boxcars left by the CPR. We'd work until the order was filled. On other days after work, I was doing everything I could to quicken the completion of Mary's house, because Cil and I were hoping we'd be into it before the baby was born. The outside walls and roof were in place, so I was working on partitions, insulation, ceiling tiles, and wall panelling.

When we had time together, Cil and I would go for a drive or pack a lunch and go for a walk into the hills south of the village so that she could get enough exercise and deliver a healthy baby—and to get away from the alcohol abuse that was rampant in the community. People were drowning their pain in alcohol; it had become a way of life for most of them. I had realistic fears of becoming an alcoholic.

On one of our Sunday drives, we spotted a huge black bear sitting underneath an apple tree below Dad's hayfield south of the main community. I had my rifle with me, in hopes of spotting a young buck. The gun didn't have a scope; it was open-sight. I used the hood of the car as a rest, took a deep breath, and pulled the trigger. The bear flopped forward from its sitting position.

We drove the car home and took the back trail to the hayfield. The bear was lying just below the apple tree. I was amazed to find that I had shot it right between the eyes. I always knew I was a good shot, but didn't know I could be that accurate. I told Cil it was going to be difficult convincing people that I had shot the bear from the highway, clear across the slough to The Point, and hit it between the eyes. That only happens to people with scopes mounted on high-powered rifles.

"Is there film in the camera?" I asked her.

"Yes."

"I want you to take a picture of me holding up the bear and pointing at the bullet hole."

That was a mistake because, traditionally, a pregnant woman must not be around a freshly killed animal. I try to remain positive about it by realizing that the spirit of the bear was automatically inherited by my first-born son, Chris, who has a laid-back, gentle bear nature about him. My brother-in-law Sam Ignatius and my sister Mary agreed to skin the bear and cut up the meat for roasts and smoke-dried jerky.

The people in the village and my co-workers at the sawmill were all counting the days until the birth, taking bets much like in a hockey pool as to what would be the date of birth, the baby's sex and weight. (In the end, Don Kepke was the closest. He said it would be a boy at eight pounds born between October 11 and 19. I figured he won because Cil and I would often have dinner with him and his wife, Mildred, during those last few weeks.

We were getting close to the time of birth when the phone rang one morning before eight. It was Ed Richter of Richter Auto Body.

"Good morning, Chris! I tried several times yesterday to get in touch, but your phone was busy."

Fall 1969—A happy moment: me with our first-born, Chris Luke, Jr. (Buck).

"I started working at the Huscroft mill, so you wouldn't have been able to get me," I said.

"So you're at the mill, eh?"

"I've been there about two months now, and I'm staying."

"Oh, I was calling to see if you wanted to come and work on a steady basis beginning this coming Monday."

"I'd say yes if I wasn't working at the mill, but the pay is great and I'm going to be a daddy soon. I'll have to turn the chance down."

After I hung up, I said to Cecilia, "I probably just turned down the one and only chance I'll ever have of doing something in the auto body trade."

I wondered if I was doing the right thing. I was hoping the decision didn't come back to haunt me.

As October was winding down, we weren't visiting or travelling as much. On the morning of the 24th, I was preparing to go to work when Cil told me she was beginning to feel periodic pain. I told her to get herself ready and I would drop her at the hospital. She checked herself in, and I hugged her and told her I would be back during lunch break.

It was a slow morning for me at work. I kept wondering how Cil was doing. At lunch hour I jumped into the car and took off for the hospital. I found her wandering in the hallway.

"How are you doing?" I asked.

"The pain is still the same. Nothing has changed."

We visited in her room in the maternity ward for

awhile and I headed back to work. "See you tonight," I said.

I couldn't wait for the day to end. Rudy and I got cleaned up after work and had supper at the Club Cafe. I left him downtown and headed for the hospital. Cil was lying in bed.

"The contractions are a lot closer, and the pain isn't as bad as before," she said.

I visited until eight p.m. when visiting hours were over. I decided to hit the sack early and took the phone off the hook because people kept calling to borrow money or ask for a ride home from the bar. I wasn't up to answering.

Early in the morning, I was awakened by loud banging on the door. It was Zach and Mary Basil. They had been trying to get hold of me. "Congratulations!" they said. "You're a father. You have a son! He was born about half an hour ago."

I was so thrilled I wanted to visit right away, but the morning was taking forever to turn into afternoon when I would be able to see Cil and our precious new little boy. (Visiting hours started at two p.m.) I woke Rudy to tell him he was an uncle again. I paced around the house wondering what the baby looked like, how Cil was doing because it had been eighteen hours since the labour started. I made myself some porridge with brown sugar. I shared the good news with Aunt Nancy. She was happy for us and she had some good advice.

"It's nice for you to be able to look after and raise your own child. When you bring the baby home from the hospital, don't coop him up in the house too much. Take him out for walks and rides so his understanding of the environment isn't limited. Especially, keep him around people so he will become a gentle, likeable person."

Then I knocked on the Louies' door and walked in.

"Guess what! I'm a daddy! My son was born around six this morning."

Robert and I headed into town to have lunch. I bought some flowers and a card for Cil. This was unfamiliar territory for me, being a proud new father. I was relishing the hype and attention I was getting. Cil took me to the nursery to see my son. Christopher Gerald Luke Jr. (Buck) weighed eight pounds ten ounces and was twenty-one inches long. I just stood looking at him for the longest time; no words would come out of my mouth. "I'm so proud," I said, "that I can't even find the words to express how I feel."

I noticed that the baby had a somewhat cone-shaped head. "Why is his head that shape? And why is he still bloody-looking?" I asked Cil.

"He was just born. That's the way they look for the first couple of days."

In amazement I stood there watching Chris Jr.'s every move, every flinch. I began to wonder what he was going to be like once he started walking and talking. I thought of my own life and my traditional upbringing. How was I going to pass my teachings on to my son?

I remembered growing up with all the horses, and how I knew each horse by name. I told Chris I would buy him a horse when he was old enough to look after one and ride on his own. Morning baths and walking and running must become a way of life for my son. Hunting would require some teaching in order for him to understand and practise the patience he had inherited. I told myself I would involve him in sports, especially in hockey, which I loved and played to the best of my ability. As I saw it, Chris Jr. was going to get the best of both the Native and non-Native worlds.

I spent the rest of that Saturday afternoon and evening with my wife and new son. On the way home I stopped by the Park Store to talk to the owners, Herman and Ida Becker. They congratulated me and told me to bring the baby by so they could see him. (Cil and I later got to be real friends with Herman and Ida. We stopped by the store often to pick up emergency items.) I bought my usual bottle of Coke and bag of Cheezies. "I'd better get home and hit the sack so I can visit Cil tomorrow," I said.

However, I was no sooner in the house than Stanley White came to the door. "Heard you had a baby boy!" he said. "Irene and I want you to come over and have a celebration drink with us."

I was hesitant. "Well, I don't really know if I want to do that right now."

"Come on, just one drink with us," urged Stanley.

In most cases, that one drink leads to another and another until you're so far gone that it doesn't matter anymore. It happened to me that night. I had good intentions, but whenever my glass was empty, Stanley or Irene would refill it with rum and Coke. When we finished the bottle of rum, we cracked open the beer. I don't remember when I went home. In fact, I didn't go to see Cil and Chris Jr. the next day, because by that time I was partying with everyone else on the reservation who had a drinking problem.

On Monday I was to begin evening shift. The hospital called in the morning to tell me that Cil and the baby could come home. I prepared myself to pick her up and face the music for not visiting on Sunday.

She asked, "What happened yesterday?"

"It's a long story."

"Long story, right," she said. "Why don't you say that the booze got the best of you? It controlled you."

That was all I needed—the truth thrown in my face. We had a few angry words. I finally apologized.

If there was such a thing as a "big mistake," that was it. You do celebrate when a child is born, but not in the fashion I did. The way I celebrated my first-born was absolutely not the way to honour a child's birth. It was the first and last time I did anything like that; I was present for the rest of our children when they were born.

I struggle with the thought of that "no-show" weekend every time a new grandchild is born into the Luke family or when any child is born into the community.

I knew then, in October of 1969, that my dependency on alcohol was a problem, but I was too proud to admit I was becoming an alcoholic. I went to the sawmill that afternoon after Cil and Chris Jr. came home, but I couldn't focus on my work.

17

ROOTS

WHILE WE WERE WORKING ON THE NEXT GROUP OF new homes, we lost one of our elders tragically to suicide. We heard one day that Nicholas Francis was in hospital. He died of a gunshot wound within a few hours.

My Uncle David, my mother's brother, was a distant relative to Nick Francis and a very good friend. People asked me how to get hold of him to tell him the bad news. David was living in Elmo, Montana, but didn't have a telephone. I called the Indian police detachment in Elmo and asked specifically for Louis Caye, who I knew would deliver the message. I told Louis to tell my uncle I would pick him up in Elmo the following day. Cil was coming with me, and I told Robert if he wanted to come he had to be at the house by eight a.m.

The three of us were on our way early. We stopped at the 3-Mile junction north of Bonners to gas up. Three and a half hours later we were in Kalispell and heading south toward Elmo, which was another hour's drive.

When we got there, Uncle David had his blue suitcase ready. He was grinning from ear to ear and giggling up a storm, like a little boy waiting to get on a merry-go-round. We started immediately for home, gassed up again, and picked up some potato chips and pop to tide us over. With my uncle telling us stories all the way, we were back in Creston before we knew it, eating supper at the Club Cafe.

Nick Francis and my uncle had grown up together. One of their most important functions was performing healing medicine dances for the benefit of the people of our community. After we buried Nick, Uncle David decided to stay for a couple of weeks because I couldn't leave to drive him home again without putting in some time at work.

Summer 1969—Robert Louie and I getting ready to take a drive somewhere.

The weekend after the funeral, he taught me how to build a sweat lodge. He taught me the significance of the sweat—to purify the lodge, mind, and spirit, so that a person has a new sense of self. The sweatlodge ceremony allows a release of the negativity that would keep a person from growing mentally and spiritually. Uncle David taught me how to respect it. He said he would pray over the lodge and we would christen it on Sunday.

I picked up sheets and blankets at a secondhand store and found an old canvas tent to use as the covering. We collected lava-forged, pitted stones up Kid Creek, and I cut some wood with a small chainsaw. Uncle David used thirty stones, and I still use that number for my sweat lodge ceremonies today. We piled the wood and placed the stones on top and put more wood in a circle to cover the stones.

On Sunday morning, he said prayers. He gave me the honour of lighting the fire. We watched as the fire took hold, burning in a circular fashion, bright and very hot. This sweat was special to me, as it was my first time since the spring of 1962. As we sat there, I knew I had to ask the question about my father. I told Uncle David that my three older sisters, Clara, Mary, and Pauline had mentioned something to me after Mom passed away, but they didn't tell me the whole truth, and maybe I didn't want to know then. But lately, I had become curious.

"So I need to know now. Who was my father?"

Uncle David didn't hesitate. "Your dad's white," he said. "His name was Bill Rohacs. He died a long time ago. I don't know what year. A tractor flipped on him and crushed him—he died right away. His dad's name was George. George hired

Native people to work his orchard—they liked him. Your mom got together with Bill when she was working, picking raspberries and cherries."

Hearing the truth hurt. Why was I not my father's son? I loved Sam, and I felt betrayed.

"Where was Dad?" I asked.

"The person you call Dad was not around—Sam Luke was in jail. He was riding his horse home from work one day. A friend of his stole a shirt and pants from a store, and he stopped Sam and asked him to hang on to them and he would get them later."

Uncle David told me that Dad didn't ask any questions, just put the shirt and pants in his saddlebag and continued to ride home. The Provincial Police stopped him and asked if he had anything in his saddlebag, because they had questioned the thief, the so-called friend, and he told them Sam Luke had a new pair of pants and a shirt. Sam said yes, he had a shirt and pants. He was charged with theft and spent eighteen months in Okalla.

After I moved the half-burned pieces of wood to the top of the fire in a circle fashion, I continued to sit quietly and listen to the story of Mom, Dad, and my mother's boyfriend, Bill. My uncle went on to tell me that Sophie visited Sam in jail, but she was angry with him for hanging on to the shirt and pants in the first place. They had harsh words, and my mother said she didn't want to see him when he got out of jail. She had no one at home because my sisters were all in residential school, so she lived with her father and step-mother. During the picking season, she lived in the pickers' shack at Washout Creek.

"This is how Sophie was with Bill. You were born after Sam came out of jail," said Uncle David.

"That's it?"

"That's it."

By this time, the wood had burned clean and the stones were glowing red. It was time to push the stones into the pit.

The next week I drove Uncle David to Bonners Ferry to catch the Greyhound back to Elmo. "I'd like to come back in a month," he said.

"That would be nice. I would like you around," I said. I loved my uncle. He was the only living survivor on my mother's side.

18

GROWING UP

CHRIS JR. WAS PROBABLY THREE WEEKS OLD WHEN WE moved our belongings to the new house. It took two days with Christine, Joan, and Florine Louie and Ida Francis giving us a hand. When we finished, Cil and I treated our helpers to hamburgers at Dairy Queen and later, beer.

That fall we continued to take little trips out of town, often to Cranbrook to see Joe and Sophie or to Trail to visit Cil's sister, Lydia, who worked at the Terra Nova Hotel, and her boyfriend Alex, who worked at Columbia Glass. We usually ended up in car lots, checking out the used vehicles, especially pickup trucks. I've always had a thing for pickup trucks. We didn't mind the Pontiac, and it was excellent on gas, but on a trip to Trail with Albert Ignatius and Robert, the car started acting up, as if it wasn't getting any gas. It finally choked and quit. Luckily, Albert knew a thing or two about engines. He said a piece of material from the air filter was stuck in the carburetor. He removed it and turned the air filter upside down—no problem.

When I found a 1962 six-cylinder gray Chev pickup with

1969—Joe and Sophie Pierre visiting us from Cranbrook, B.C.

a short wide box at the GM dealership in Creston, I decided to try and sell the Pontiac.

"Are you interested in buying your old car back?" I asked Zach.

"Are you serious?"

"No, just joking," I said. "Do you know anyone who might be interested in a nice car?"

"Leave it with me. I'll check around."

And that was how I met Ray Aasen, who was a friend of Zach's and just starting a business, Ray's Garbage Pick-Up. He owned a small acreage in Lister, a field of alfalfa that he cut and stored for sale. He was interested in taking a look at the Pontiac sometime. Neither of us was in any rush. I wanted to use it for hunting that fall. "Drive it by when you can," he said.

When I finally did show him the car, he was impressed with the shape it was in, especially the engine. After he took it for a drive, he said he would buy it. With the cash, I was able to put a down payment on the pickup; working at the mill was security enough to get me a six-month payment plan.

I wanted to give my truck a face-lift—maybe some rims and tires with character. Not one of the tire stores had the rims I wanted, so I thought of Brennan's Garage out in Erickson. Sometimes Earl Brennan had supplies that the other shops didn't carry. Sure enough, he found some chrome rims, six-hole! So $75 later, I was the proud owner of a set of chrome rims and baby moon caps that Earl had found in the original box. He said he had ordered them for a fellow who never came to pick them up. With the new equipment and the tool box that Ike Basil had built for me, my truck was looking priceless.

As it got colder, ice was being made for curling at the Erickson packing shed. Ken Huscroft wanted to put a team together and asked Ozzie, Joe, and myself if we'd like to curl. I had never curled before so I played lead; Joe was second, Ozzie third, and Ken was skip. I actually enjoyed the game. Curling takes skill, concentration, and wit. We attended the Huscroft mill Christmas party, inviting Joe and Sophie to join us.

That Christmas of 1969, Cil and I spent a lot of time shopping for gifts. It was the first time we were shopping for one another and her family back in Vernon. She packaged all the presents in one big box and sent them to Vernon by Greyhound.

On Christmas Eve, we decided to go to Midnight Mass at the Catholic Church in Creston. Father Morelli was conducting the Mass. We arrived at the church a half hour before the service, but the only room left was in the middle of the second row from the front. Cil and I were ushered in, and we had to excuse ourselves as we made our way to sit down. I carried the baby, who was two months old, and Cil carried the baby bag. As I glanced around, I noticed that all of the eyes in the congregation were focused on us. I had flashbacks of my first day of school.

I suppose we presented a strange picture. I suppose those people were experiencing culture shock. We were already stereotyped as lazy and a bunch of drunks, and it wasn't the thing for Native people to go to church and worship the birth of Jesus Christ. As it turned out, Chris Jr. started to act up about three-quarters of the way through the Mass. So we left, and we've never gone back to church except for weddings and funerals.

I told Cil we would bring in the New Year traditionally, just the three of us. On New Year's Eve I took my rifle out. At ten minutes before midnight, Cil bundled up our son and we went outside. As my dad used to do, I said a prayer in Ktunaxa; I thanked the Creator for the past year, for a beautiful wife and child, for all the gifts given through spirituality. I prayed for the coming year, that it be just as prosperous as the last, and I fired three shots towards the east to welcome the new days and nights. Then I turned to Cil and Chris Jr. and hugged them. We celebrated with a snack of crackers, cheese, garlic meats, and pop. I went back to work at the mill on the first Monday in 1970.

News that the mill would shut down for maintenance during spring breakup in April prompted Cil and I to make plans to visit her family in Vernon. We invited Robert (he was in grade twelve) to go with us, as he also had a week off. We were meeting Lydia and Alex in Castlegar, then travelling via Slocan, Nakusp, and Lumby. I found the route treacherous and almost plunged over the edge at one spot that was single-lane traffic and blind at the other end. It seemed that the road vanished, except that it made a quick right in the rock cut. The trip seemed endless, but it actually took only five and a half hours.

Cil's mom was excited to see her new grandson, and Cil was only interested in visiting with family. I wanted to see Jerry and introduce Robert to some of the guys. He already knew Earl and Pearl Tonasket, Willard's brother and sister. He had met them at the Sardis hospital for controlling tuberculosis when he was a patient there for a couple of months.

As I expected, Jerry was picking away at his guitar when we arrived. I made my way downstairs and hollered, "Hey, *slaux*, it's me! I'm here to visit. Put your toy away."

I introduced him to Robert and we sat over coffee. I was thinking how wonderful it was to be at that table chatting with family, as many as four conversations going on at the same time. I found out that Jerry was still working at Hilltop Auto Wreckers.

"Where's Willard?" I asked.

"He's around. Still travels back and forth to Oroville...Hey, let's go for a ride to show your buddy around, see if Willard's home, and take a drive to Enderby."

The three of us—Jerry, Robert, and I—jumped into Jerry's car and headed for Six-Mile Creek on the west side of the Okanagan Indian Reservation. I explained to Robert that the reserve was six times larger than ours in Creston, with ten times the population. We picked up Willard and Henry Wilson and cruised around for hours doing what young men of twenty-two enjoy doing—yelling at girls on the street and going for Chinese food, which Jerry and I paid for. At that time, it cost $1.25 per plate. Jerry wanted to have a jam session. Without thinking, I agreed, but I had to back out when I realized that I was a married man and had made earlier plans with my wife, who also had things she wanted to do and people she wanted to visit.

Cil and I spent a good week with friends and family, showing off our six-month-old baby boy. We left for home the following Sunday, driving back via Osoyoos. As we drove over the Salmo-Creston summit, the muffler on the truck broke away from its hanger. The only thing I had to tie it up with was a lace from my running shoe. The repair job lasted until we got to Summit Creek Park. I retied it and we were able to make the last few miles home.

When I had Alan Hughes at the Husky service station replace the clamp and hanger, I took the time to check the car lots in town. Alan had a 1967 El Camino, which he offered to sell. I asked if I could test drive the car. It was very much a "muscle" car, an automatic 396-cubic-inch with a harness shift on the floor. Robert and I took it for a spin across the flats. Then I took Cil for a ride towards Porthill.

"What do you think?" I asked her.

"I don't know. It's a little too fancy for us. We could never afford something like this."

So I had Cil's thoughts, and I decided to get Zach's opinion as well. I drove him up Mallory Road and turned around at the golf course.

"What do you think of this vehicle?" I asked again. "Would you buy it?"

"No. It's got too much power and not enough room. It's too much like a toy," he said.

I returned the El Camino to Alan and told him we were thinking about more of a family car. Cil and I started to check out the car lots in town. Because of my many visits to the Chrysler Dodge dealership, I became good friends with Theo Hendren. I would say, "Hey, Theo, what's new?" "Not too much, Chris," he would say. Then I'd say, "No, I mean in vehicles." And Theo would finish it with, "Okay, you got me again."

He showed Cil and me a sky-blue 1966 Barracuda that a fellow had traded in while driving through Creston. We fell in love with it right away. After the test drive, we liked it even more because of how it handled. It was a simple car, great on gas, had a 318-cubic-inch motor and a huge hatchback window in the rear. It was the perfect car for us.

"So what's the sale price?" I asked Theo. After he told me, I reminded him that I was working at the mill earning just a bit better than minimum wage, which was approximately $1.55 per hour at the time. "What can you do for me?"

Theo was able to give me a good deal. He reduced the sale price and took my pickup as a trade-in and down payment.

In June there was news that a second crew was being formed at the sawmill. Ken Huscroft asked me if I knew of anyone looking for work. Right away, I thought of Robert Louie and Albert Ignatius. Robert was soon to finish school and answered quickly. "Sure," he said. Albert was thinning apples but wanted a permanent job, so I told Ken I had two people lined up.

It was exciting to have them both working alongside me. We had been put on the night shift, which went from three o'clock in the afternoon until eleven-thirty, with half an hour for supper. We got home before midnight.

Since Robert was earning some money, he wanted to check out the Honda motorcycles in town that Bob Corner had in stock. Robert had his eye on a green Honda 100 that was on sale for $400. We worked out a payment plan with Bob. Zach Basil put up the initial down payment, and once Robert had made the rest of the payments, he repaid Zach.

It didn't take Robert long to get the hang of driving the motorcycle. The gear system was simple with the usual one up and three down. One day he was practising on the main road in the community. He was cat-walking the bike, but the throttle was wide open. He slipped off and was running along behind still holding on to the handlebars. I hollered, "Release the gas! Release the gas!"

Once he got used to riding, Robert would take Chris Jr.

from one end of the village to the other and drop him off in front of our house. On weekends, he rode to Naples, Idaho, "just for a ride."

After two months, I was beginning to feel the stress of night shift. The foreman, Jim Moman, told me to see Ken Huscroft about rescheduling. After that meeting, we were all back working days. What a relief. It felt great to work days again.

September 5, 1970, Labour Day weekend, was the opening day for hunting big game. On the day before, there was a lot of excitement at work, especially for the guys who were looking forward to leaving that Friday and setting up their camps. I really wanted to go hunting, but Cil thought we ought to visit her family in Vernon before the weather change made it more difficult. I agreed and we left early the next day.

As we headed out of town toward the summit, we thought it strange that there were police cars and heavily armed officers at the intersections leading to Creston, Wynndel, and West Creston. They didn't stop us, just waved us through. We thought they must be checking hunters. There was another police car at the top of the Salmo-Creston and one at the bottom at the Nelway junction. We didn't think anything more about how unusual this was.

In Trail I turned on the car radio and we heard the shocking news that a mass murder had taken place in the Creston Valley. As I listened to the early description of the incident, the location and number of victims, my first thought was of the Lower Kootenay Band. Had someone lost his cool while in a drunken state and committed murder? I was wondering how we had slept right through it. It wasn't surprising that I would be thinking this way. I was witnessing in my village the death of a people, a band, a nation that was controlled by alcohol. It had become a way of life. Anything could happen under that influence.

We returned to Creston on Labour Day Monday, to a saddened and hyped-up town, to the tragic deaths of eight members of two West Creston families. This tragedy, called the goriest in Kootenay history, had ended the day before when a thirty-year-old man was apprehended in West Creston about a hundred yards from his cabin. He was charged with non-capital murder.

The entire valley was traumatized and in mourning. I was personally in shock because I knew the man through the Creston Boxing Club. He had sparred with the younger boxers and worked out with the rest of us. I had thought of him as a person who would take the shirt off his back to help you out.

As the Creston Valley settled down and people got back to their daily routines, my thoughts turned to hunting. Alex and Lydia came over from Trail to visit on a weekend, so Alex and I spent all of Saturday and part of Sunday hunting *kyaqɫa* (ducks) and *kaxuɫuk* (geese). Part of the time, I patrolled the hunting areas for trespassers, as we'd had problems in the past with illegal hunters on the Lower Kootenay Band properties. Zach, who had been the Band manager for almost a year, asked Robert and me to notify him right away if we caught anyone without a daily or seasonal permit issued by the Band.

I did question three men who were on the band wetlands without authorization that weekend. One of them I recognized as a business owner from Creston. Zach made it a point to talk to him about trespassing and to speak with the RCMP staff sergeant, as another of the trespassers was a member of the detachment. I distinctly remember Zach telling the businessman he ought to know better, that his friends and business "we could do without." That was the only time I ever witnessed Zach being annoyed or angry with anyone. The RCMP constable received a slap on the wrist, and several months later he was transferred out of Creston.

At the end of September, George Kusiak asked me if I wanted to go hunting with him in the Wardner, Jaffray, Galloway area of the East Kootenay. We saw some game, but what we saw was not antlered. We passed the day behind the pole mill in Galloway and drove towards Elko before dark, hoping to see something with antlers. We left the main highway near the intersection that leads to the Montana border, drove a few miles south and then back towards Cranbrook, where we had supper. It was a great day that we ended with a beer at his place back in Creston.

I managed to get a young buck not far from home. Cil and I butchered it and took some fresh cuts we were going to use right away. I showed her how we prepared *wa¢kna* over a hot, smoking fire. The dry meat is similar to beef jerky.

In October the landscape began to change. The leaves were turning yellow and orange. To the west of the Lower

Kootenay community, ducks and geese were arriving flock after flock, and the waterways were thick with birds feeding, and the sandbars were covered with duck and goose droppings. This was the time of year that several of us would go hunting for ourselves and for band members who couldn't hunt anymore. We all had our favourite spots. On the flats, I was either patrolling for poachers or spotting the birds to find out where the most activity was taking place. I would also take note of the muskrat and beaver activity so I could mark the area before anyone else put their claim on it, as I was beginning to prepare my traps. We used different coloured ribbons to claim our areas, and the ribbons were acknowledged and respected without question.

At home, Chris Jr. was beginning to take a few steps. Before his first birthday, he was walking. Cil and I were so proud of how he carried himself independently; he refused to hold our hands, just wanted to be free and run along by himself.

I was happy with my little family, happy with my work, but concerned about what was happening at Yaqan Nukiy. People were dying one after the other, and most of the deaths were alcohol-related. I was also drinking too much. I didn't want to indulge, because I knew that I couldn't handle my liquor. One beer was not enough for me. I had to drink until I was inebriated, and when that happened I felt bad because usually I was not aware of what I said or did. Was I rude to people? Did I argue? As I matured, these thoughts went through my mind.

We also received word that Irene Isadore, Mary Basil's only sister, had passed away in Vancouver, losing her battle with tuberculosis. Cil and I both felt a deep sadness, especially for Mary, and Irene's husband Stanley, and the boys, Gary and Ronnie, who hadn't even begun to know their mother. Her body was transported back to Creston and the funeral service took place at St. Peter's Church on the reserve. She was buried in the Lower Kootenay community cemetery.

One day Zach and Mary asked me to drive them to Porthill for a beer. Cil and I decided it would be good for all of us to get out for a few hours. As we waited at "the bottom bar" (now called Roy's Place) for the Cal Beebe band to start playing, Zach told us that the welfare system of the B.C. government was threatening to apprehend Irene's two boys. She had contacted them before her death to request they step in if anything happened to her. Zach and Mary felt that the Band Council needed to intervene and set up a satisfactory home support service for the family in order to avoid apprehension of any kind. (Between 1963 and 1970, thirty-nine children were removed from the Yaqan Nukiy community and put into foster care.)

Zach asked if I was interested in running for Council. Nominations and an election were slated for November. "We need to think about governing ourselves. We need to do for ourselves what the Department of Indian Affairs is doing," he said. "We need new ideas and younger people."

I looked over at Cil, who was talking with Mary, and wondered what she would think of the idea. The band was finally playing and people were dancing, kicking up their heels. Pat Hambler joined us for a beer and then went back to sit with his group of friends. When Cal and the band played "Kawlija," Zach jumped up and hollered and beat his chest.

The crowd was clapping along with the music, clapping extra hard whenever Zach sang out "Kawlija!" and did his King Kong impression. Cal Beebe later asked Zach for permission to sing a song he had composed about Moses George, and Zach said, "Sure." In his younger years, Moses seemed to find trouble. The song was about a car pileup he had caused near the Dairy Queen in Creston.

I knew I was going to wake up with a headache the next day. With all the noise, it was hard to hear what Zach was saying to me about running for Band Council. I didn't mention that other people had already approached me to ask if they could nominate me. I told him I would give it some thought.

19

A NEW DIRECTION

ZACH TOLD ME THAT INDIAN AFFAIRS HAD APPROVED plans to build administrative offices in the band hall, and that he had hired Ike Basil and Wilfred Jacobs to do the work.

The more he talked about management and Council responsibility, the more interested I became. He asked Cil if she had any experience typing and working with numbers, because he had put together a budget that included hiring a secretary. She told him she had Typing 10 and Bookkeeping 10. I wondered how Cil was feeling about all this and about my running for Band Council. Was she ready to share me, to accept the changes that would take place, to take the inevitable criticism?

We drove Zach and Mary home at midnight after our trip to Porthill. He was leaving in the morning for Kamloops to participate in the Union of British Columbia Indian Chiefs Conference. Chief Basil had delegated Zach to attend on behalf of the Lower Kootenay Band.

I did have a heck of a headache at work. The day dragged. When I got home, Cil told me that Zach had been in an accident near Canal Flats, that he had struck a cement bridge abutment and received severe head injuries. Mary was on her way to see him in the hospital in Windermere. He was pronounced dead the next day, October 6, 1970.

His sudden death was a blow to many of us. Zach had been very vocal and dedicated to the betterment of the Lower Kootenay community. He attacked the many problems facing us with diligence. I had shared my dreams and aspirations with Zach Basil. I saw him as an older brother, someone I could talk with when things got to be a bit too much for me. He had said to me, "It can happen for you just as long as you keep it simple and within reality." During the funeral service and burial, I developed a wall of numbness that I cannot seem to break.

Cil kept asking me how I felt about running for Band Council, whether I would be able to handle it. I made up my mind to run, but I never did ask her if she agreed with my choice.

I told George about my decision at work and he said, "Well, you said you were going to be chief someday. This is your chance to do it."

The nominations meeting took place on November 3, with elections slated for November 10. Dave Powell was the official from the Department of Indian Affairs in Cranbrook, a sub-office of the Kootenay-Okanagan District in Vernon. About twelve people were at the meeting. Dave explained the process, and then he opened the floor for nominations.

Florine Louie had taken me aside to ask again if I would let my name stand for Council. I said yes, and she told me she would nominate me for Chief. Pauline Luke was going to second it. I felt a bit overwhelmed by the whole thing.

Nominated for Chief, one to be elected, were Isaac Basil and myself. Nominated for councillor positions, two to be elected, were Mary Basil, Pete White, and Stanley White. Dave called out three times, "Are there any further nominations?" and declared the meeting closed. Five of us were running for three positions. The term was for two years.

After the meeting Dave told me he would post notices of nomination at the band hall and in a public place (the Creston Post Office), and place one with the newspaper.

"So what are the responsibilities of being chief of this community?" I asked him.

"The powers and responsibilities vary from one band to another, according to custom and tradition. Your character will play a part in the role you assume. Generally, there are certain duties that go along with being chief."

He proceeded to read the duties to me from a scribbler he had with him: to act as spokesperson for the Band at all meetings and official functions; to express opinions and feelings as an individual and for band members dealing with matters of concern regarding the Band; to make decisions individually in times of emergency, but always make known to Band Council the decisions made; to call special meetings of Band Council for business matters that cannot wait for the next regular meeting of Council; to act as chairman of Band Council meetings and only vote in the case of a tie.

"Chris, you're young and I believe you can handle it,"

Dave said. "If you're going to campaign, I know you'll make a good leader. Good luck. See you next week."

The balance of the week went on forever. I was so excited, I was constantly pacing like a kid waiting for an ice cream cone. When I finally settled down, reality set in. Cil warned, "Don't forget that you're running for chief, and it's going to take more than talking to make an impression with the band members. Remember, no promises!"

At work, I told George what had happened. "Good for you," he said. "What are you going to do when you need to go away for conferences and meetings?"

"I haven't thought that far ahead," I answered. "I'm not chief yet."

I was feeling excited but afraid at the same time—afraid of rejection, afraid of the unknown, afraid of the responsibilities that went along with the title of Chief. Tuesday morning, November 10, was such a special day. It changed my simple life to one of complexity.

During lunch break I drove home from the mill to vote. I assured Dave I would be there during the ballot count in the evening. After work I raced home, had supper, and was at the band hall at six o'clock when the election officially closed. Dave counted the ballots for Chief first and then the ballots for Councillors.

I became the newly elected Chief; Mary Basil and Stan White were elected as Councillors. I was in awe. I felt wonderful and fearful at the same time. Those who were there during the ballot count, including Ike Basil, the outgoing Chief, congratulated me.

George Huscroft laughed when I told him the news. "See,

I told you you could do it! So what are you going to do about work? To be a good chief, you can't be piling boards at the mill."

I knew George was right, and I had been thinking about applying for the Band manager position. In the middle of December, the new council met with Dave Powell and the Kootenay-Okanagan district manager, George Barrett, who congratulated us on our success in the election. He spoke about the ongoing lease agreements and financial agreements. The Lower Kootenay Band was one of the first in British Columbia to administer the programs and services from the Department of Indian Affairs. I definitely wanted the opportunity to carry out the policies.

The district manager said he would be back in a couple of weeks to finalize the Band manager position. "In the meantime," he said, "read up on the Indian Act and let me know what you think of it."

The main purpose of the Indian Act was and is to control and regulate the lives of "Indians." It consists of policies and procedures written for Status First Nations people to comply with while living on the reservation, and for Band Councils to administer their day-to-day activities, rules, and regulations. As it stands today, First Nations people are still the wards of the federal government.

I was beginning to look more closely at some of my people, and I saw oppression, pain, repressed anger. With all the other discriminations, they were not allowed to vote or to own large tracts of land. I wasn't yet fully aware of the control and influence the Department of Indian Affairs held over us; the fact that without its administration and program dollars for education and economic development, we would not be able to provide services to our people. I didn't consider then that we could have been much more self-supporting and less dependent on Indian Affairs had they honoured their fiduciary obligation as prescribed in the Indian Act. Because of this control and our dependency, our non-Indian friends and neighbours and the white public in general had a ticket to continue to discriminate against us. For them to insinuate that *their* tax dollars were being spent by my people was and still is derogatory and ludicrous.

It wasn't until later that I started asking questions. When has Canada ever paid the Indian people for the removal of this land's resources, the forests, minerals, for the exploitation of our water resources, fish, air? How could the Canadian people allow their government to exploit me and my ancestors, to allow institutions to draft laws against my people and then encourage and promote them? How do you define equality when none is shown?

When the district manager returned, I signed the Band manager agreement that would expire in December of 1976. I felt relieved knowing I had a job for the next five years, without interruption. I met with Ken Huscroft to tell him the good news and to give him my verbal resignation. I was officially finished working at the mill on December 23, 1970.

Before Christmas I hosted a dinner and dance to give thanks for the honour of becoming the leader and Chief of the Band. In the Ktunaxa tradition, this means putting your food up for a feast and gaining spiritual strength to lead and represent your people in an honourable and respectable way.

Uncle David reminded me of the importance of this tradition, and he said I needed to talk to a leader who would speak on my behalf, who knew the ways and would "traditionally stand me up," a ceremony similar to a swearing-in. He told me to ask Chief Eneas Abraham, hereditary chief from Bonners Ferry, to do the honours. Chief Abraham said he would be happy to do it.

My uncle prepared the sweat lodge for the ceremony to take place before the feast and dance. Chief Abraham was my honoured guest and ceremonial speaker. The whole community attended, and I invited several of my newfound friends: Ken and Gloria Huscroft, Roy and Joyce Johnson from Yahk, and co-workers from the mill. A few of the guys came for dinner and listened to Chief Abraham, who spoke in Ktunaxa. He spoke about the process of "standing up" a leader, about the responsibilities and hardships I would encounter. He turned his attention to band members and reminded them of their responsibility to assist me wherever possible. I did my best to translate for the English speakers. After the speeches, as my co-workers left, they came up to me one by one to shake my hand and congratulate me.

I put on my regalia and the dancing began in minipowwow style. We danced until two in the morning. My son Chris danced so hard that his legs were sore the next day.

Uncle David told me my life would be taking a big turn and that it would not be my own anymore. I was twenty-two years old and, like everything else, I took his words lightly. I did not consider how much my life would change, that I would need to become responsible, accountable, committed. I would experience confusion and loneliness. I would become bitter and verbally abusive at times, lashing out at my wife and laying blame.

I did not consider the abuses, the obstacles, the social pressures, the effects and stresses on my body and spirit that I would face in this leadership role during the next twenty-two years. But, with my growing confidence and humble style, I took on the role of Chief. Through thick and thin, I earned the trust and respect of my peers.

EPILOGUE

I BEGAN WRITING ABOUT MY LIFE SEVERAL YEARS AGO, in the fall of 1992 to be exact, right after my retirement dinner. Not pushing myself, I would write a bit and then leave it for a few weeks. In fact, I didn't touch my book for a couple of years. One morning I picked up my scribbler and started writing again.

I ran into Dr. Dave Perrin one day in 2001. He had written and published his own book about his experiences as a veterinarian in Creston Valley. We talked about writing and how hard it was to get down to it. Dave told me I had a story to tell and maybe I should put everything else aside, quit being lazy, and start writing. He contacted Betsy Brierley, who had edited his book, and asked her if she'd be interested in editing my material. She agreed to look at it.

A month after she started on my book, Betsy and I had a dinner meeting at the Other Side café. She showed me several places where she suggested I give more detail. I began to talk about what I was trying to bring across to the reader. As I was speaking, Betsy was looking at me in the way someone looks when they are ready to pop a question, but not right at that moment. She waited for me to finish, then said, "In chapter three, you mention that it was much later that you discovered your true identity. What was it? And when were you going to mention it in the book?"

Oh no! I knew how emotional I got when I thought about my identity. The many years of uncertainty, the pain, the hurt it caused my mother and me, my adopted father, my sisters and brother. My family was made to feel shame because of me. I remembered one occasion when my mother and Sam had an argument about me; it didn't sound pretty, and I immediately had that unwanted feeling.

"It isn't something I can talk openly about," I said. But I tried to explain it and described the process that brought me to this point. I told her that under the Indian Act and Indian Affairs registry I would be considered an illegitimate child. It was because Sam Luke signed the paternal document accepting me as his son that I became a member of the Lower Kootenay Band. I looked to him as a very honourable man with a big heart. "I'm proud to call him Dad."

"I think you need to decide if you want to write about it," Betsy said. She thought that it would give an understanding of some of the hardship I went through. In any case, I would need to explain my identity or not mention it at all.

I told her I needed to get hold of a woman named Jean, Matilda Hubner's daughter, because my biological father, Bill, was her uncle. She would be able to tell me more about him. Betsy told me her husband had helped to organize his fortieth high school reunion, and that Jean Hubner had graduated in that class of 1960. We were both surprised at this connection. She told me who to contact to get an address and maybe a telephone number.

On that same day, June 7, 2001, I did find an address and Jean's married name. She was my first cousin. I was so nervous I had to get Cil to phone directory assistance for the phone number.

Then I only had to make the call. I paced back and forth between the living room and the dining room. I felt sick, nauseated. I didn't want to pick up the phone. I was like a little kid wanting to surprise a friend he hasn't seen in a long time. I finally dialled.

"Hello, is this Jean?"

"Yes, I'm Jean," the woman said.

"My name is Chris Luke. You don't know me, but I believe we are related. My father was Bill Rohacs, your uncle. Do you know who I'm talking about?"

"Yes, William was my uncle."

"Jean, I should tell you I'm of First Nations ancestry. I live in Creston and I'm Chief of the Lower Kootenay Band. I hope that this is not a shock to you."

She said it wasn't a shock, but that she didn't know her Uncle Bill had a son in Creston. "I appreciate this call, Chris."

There was a moment of silence. I didn't say anything. I was trying to picture the woman at the other end of the line. Did she look like her mother? I was still nervous. I blurted out that I had been diagnosed with diabetes and that the doctor advised me to notify my family because it was a hereditary condition. Jean said she wasn't aware of anyone in her family having diabetes. I said I had probably screwed up my own system, and I continued to ask her questions.

"Do you have any other family?"

She told me she had aunts and cousins. She said I had a half-sister by the name of Dianne somewhere, but she didn't know where, and she didn't know what her last name was now.

I was speechless. Was this a dream? When I could find words, I said, "Jean, if you ever cross paths with her, please let her know she has a brother. Give her my address and telephone number."

Jean also told me one of her aunts had a photograph of my father, Bill, in his uniform. He had served in the army from 1941 to 1945. "Maybe she can send you a picture."

"That would be great," I said. "I would certainly appreciate it...I should let you go, Jean, and if you see your family let them know that I called."

Before she hung up she told me to stay in touch.

"I will," I said. "You really made this evening special for me by talking to me."

I hung up the phone. I was trembling inside; the feeling was overwhelming. I was so excited I could not sit down. I paced back and forth as I told Cil about the conversation.

While I was pacing, a vehicle stopped in our driveway. It was my friend, John Kettle, who had come to discuss some outstanding business. We go back to the mid-1970s. He used to come up from Texas to hunt in what is now the Lower Kootenay Band guiding territory. He knocked on the door and walked in.

"What's wrong?" he asked, when he saw my face. "You look like you've seen a ghost!"

I shared my news with him.

"Man! I wouldn't have known the difference, Chris. You look very much Native to me."

"Well, to a lot of people I do, and to some I don't."

We sat in silence for a few minutes before we got down to our business. When he got up to leave, he said, "Maybe sometime soon I'll have a sweat bath with you." He laughed and said, "You've had me sweating all week." Then we both laughed.

The next day I sat with Cil at lunch. "It's a relief," I told her. "I don't have to wonder about my white side anymore."

On the other hand, I felt naked. My secret was out. Unless people have experienced that uncertainty, the mental and emotional anguish, they can never know what I've had to live with. Although I called Sam Luke my father and became very close to him, historically the people of Yaqan Nukiy have separated me from him. Only a few acknowledged the father/son relationship that we had.

I've tried to put it all behind me, and finding the other half of my identity has enabled me to do just that. I no longer have to live with the ridicule and shame of being illegitimate, a bastard. I did have a father; in fact, I had two fathers.

In the weeks that followed, I was actually in touch with the aunt that Jean talked about and with my sister, Dianne. I found out, too, that Dianne and I have a half-sister living in Holland.

I began to think that maybe writing about my roots would help me get past the pain and anger, and I could live with the wonderful, fond memories of my upbringing within the Lower Kootenay community. I believe I have made the best of both worlds. Learning the traditions and cultural values of the

Native way and adapting to non-Native traditions and values have increased my self-awareness. I am proud of who I am and what I stand for. I am able to communicate and interact as an individual, but especially as a member of Yaqan Nukiy.

In September my son Chris wanted to have a sweat before he left for Chicago to run an eight-week hockey school. He had done it the year before and was very successful, so the organization wanted him to run another one. My son Chad and grandson Colton came by to build the fire to heat the stones in the sweat lodge. In a little over an hour, the stones were ready.

In my opening prayer I thanked the Creator for everything in my life path—the rocks and the sweat lodge, the ground we walk on, the air and the water, the food on the table, the clothes on my back, the roof over my head, my language, my health, and my wife, children, grandchildren, friends, enemies, and all my people.

"Thank you for the spiritual gifts of prayer, vision, and the healing power. Thank you for my son, who requested this sweat. Thank you for this wonderful day and making it possible for me to find my roots."

About the Author

KAKA NU⅃KIN K⅃AW⅃AS (Drags Grizzly/Chris Luke) is a member of the Ktunaxa Nation. He was born in the old Creston Valley Hospital and raised in the village of Yaqan Nukiy on the Lower Kootenay reservation in southeast British Columbia.

At present, he is the elected Chief of the Lower Kootenay Band, a position he first held at the age of twenty-two. He began writing his story in 1992 after stepping down from leadership. He also initiated his own consulting and facilitation business, delivering workshops and programs on community growth and awareness.

His relentless commitment and dedication to his people

and community have given him gifts that he shares unselfishly—and he continues to live and practise his beliefs in a traditional, gentle, and humble way.

He resides in the community of Yaqan Nukiy with his wife and family. He is currently working on his second book.